Praise for *No F*

"By holding a palpable tens[...] [ex]periences and the mystery of [near-death] encounters, Joyce has woven a story that enthralls and inspires. Her clarity and courage allow us to glimpse the numinous."

DIANE MARSHALL, MA, Registered Clinical Counsellor, co-founder of B.C. Brain (Head) Injury Association, Director of Caring Circle

"Joyce Ganong has written an extraordinary book. She vividly recalls and describes exactly what is happening to her and her body, at a level of detail that transports the reader into the situation, while at the same time retaining an ethereal, spiritual perspective that transcends space and time. I enjoyed—no, *devoured*—this book, in which Joyce has truly reassured her readers that Death is not to be feared, and that Life is meant to be filled with love.... That is her legacy and I am changed by having read her story."

CAROL MACKINNON, MA, Leadership Coach, co-author of *Leadership Alchemy: The Magic of the Leader Coach*

"Joyce paints amazingly vivid word pictures. I can see, feel, taste, and smell each and every experience. It is as if I am there with her through every step of the journey. And what an incredible journey it is. A very sensuous and deeply spiritual trip. This is a very moving and courageous book that is hard to put down."

SHIRLEY ROBERTSON, MA, former Regional Director, Government of Canada

"An intimate and compelling chronicle of life-threatening acute illness interrupting a special anniversary celebration in Tuscany, and the treatment and recovery punctuated by exquisite and liminal cross-cultural adventures, all wrapped in a tender and enduring love story. A rare and bold personal sharing usually reserved only for voicing in the second or third person."

MORRIS FLEWWELLING, CM, AOE, LLD, FCMA

My hospital adventure in Tuscany

Joyce Ganong

Joyce Ganong (signature)

NO

FEAR

IN

DEATH'S

LIGHT

FAULKS BRIDGE

PRESS

Faulks Bridge Press
Bowen Island, Canada

Catalogue data available from Library and Archives Canada
ISBN 978-0-9952569-0-3 (print)
ISBN 978-0-9952569-1-0 (ebook)

Editing by Shirarose Wilensky
Cover and text design by Peter Cocking

16 17 18 19 20   5 4 3 2 1

— For Lael —

PREFACE

I N SEPTEMBER 2012, Gordon and I were on our twenty-fifth wedding anniversary celebration trip.

We had started our marriage in mid-life. I was a package deal with my daughters, Michelle and Susan. When Gordon said, "I do," he was making his commitment to them as well as to me. With pride we watched as they established their own full lives: Michelle, a family lawyer focussed on the needs of children as their parents divorced; Susan, a middle school teacher and mom to Ella and Finn. Oh my—those two wee ones! Already such unique personalities filled with fun and love. The icing on our life cake.

Yes, our life together had been full—well worth celebrating.

And everything was made more poignant by our dawning realization that life is short. We had reached the age when deaths were occurring all around us. Just that past June, our dear friend Philip had died. Cancer reduced that hearty, fun-filled, curious, intellectual man to dust, leaving Marnie—his soulmate and wife of nearly fifty years—bereft, anchorless. We missed him. We ached for her. We missed them.

So we were well aware that our time together was precious. This trip was just for the two of us, for remembering, for living each moment, for building new memories, for enjoying time with one another.

Although we stopped in Paris and Florence along the way, the major focus of our trip was to be the countryside of Tuscany—the land of light, olive groves and vineyards, local produce and cheeses, and ancient ruins. All within easy reach of our idyllic farmhouse-style apartment, short drives away from the western coastline, hilltop towns, and culinary delights.

But life has its way of surprising us, even giving us more, and less, at the same time. Our romantic vacation in Tuscany was no exception to the whims of life. Life had lessons for us there.

Within each of us are extraordinary abilities we may never know we have—deep knowledge, abnormal strength, ways of communicating other than by speaking or listening. We often discover these untapped treasures when facing life-threatening danger or trauma. It's as if the crisis lifts us into a different space where we have access to our own rich resources.

That is what happened to me.

My experience had such a profound impact on me that I was compelled to share my story with you. There are parts of my story you will believe. There are parts of my story—the parts that are unexplainable in everyday life—that you may have difficulty believing. The choice to believe or not is yours. I've simply told what I experienced and what I learned as I existed in what I call "liminal space."

COME WALK *with me in that space we share—the universal space where we are one, you and I. And from this space you will experience what I experienced, life unfolding and revealing layer upon layer of other lives and other places rarely seen. It starts in pain, but it doesn't stay there, so don't be afraid. Walk with me.*

1

SEPTEMBER 21

—————

O UR SECOND morning in Tuscany.
The roosters of the neighbouring farms compete
for our attention in that magical time just before
dawn. They are silenced only by first light and the frantic
barking of the hunting dogs anxious to track their prey—Tuscany's famed wild boar. Wakened so early, we watch as the
golden Tuscan light fills the nearby hills with glorious depth—
the olive trees emerging from the dark, dripping wet from
last evening's shower; the grapevines, heavy with dark purple grapes, steaming with promise. A glorious way to wake.

Two cups of tea later, with maps strewn about, we are excited and ready for our day: First to a coffee and pastry shop
for a true Italian breakfast. Then to Pisa. Maybe even a drive
to explore the coast—it doesn't look far. All unplanned until
today. Perfect.

But—

Jolts of excruciating pain stab through my lower gut.
Huge, molten shards of pain that burn and twist and sever

me from our morning. My new reality is only the pain and the onslaught of new shards, each more devastating than the last. Immediately, I double over, unable to remain upright, and rush to the toilet, shoving Gordon out of the bathroom as his frightened eyes take in my transformation from just minutes before. I gingerly sit on the toilet, expecting a rush of diarrhea, for surely this must be what the pain is all about.

Nothing.

No diarrhea. No blood. No urine.

Nothing.

I push, frantically hoping that I can unblock the stoppage.

Two short bursts of diarrhea.

Then nothing.

I push some more, only to guess that I've pushed my rectal muscle out through my anus. A different kind of excruciating pain. Now I'm unable to sit anywhere comfortably, even if that had been possible with those roiling, never-ending shards of pain. Still molten white, now they seem to be not only white-hot but also corrosive, taking on an evil, greenish cast as they build.

I stand and lean on the bidet across from me, my arms giving support to my doubled-over position. My head seeks and finds the cold white-tile wall. Minutes later, I notice that I am finding relief by hitting my head against the tile, at first gently. But, as the pain in my gut increases, my head is moving of its own volition, hammering the tile harder and faster, until I realize that I could give myself a concussion.

Sudden retching brings up pure unadulterated bile, staining the bidet and leaving my mouth and throat raw. Sickened by the sight and smell, I leave the bathroom.

I try to lie down on the bed, seeking a soft surface. Mistake. The contortion of my body does not permit any comfort. I move to a corner in the living room, gaining support from the two sturdy walls, and take two Dicetel, a prescription I have for cramps in my bowel. I'll try anything.

Finally, I ask Gordon to get help. This pain is not going away; in fact, it seems to be increasing. "How can that be?" I think.

He rushes down the twenty uneven terra cotta tile steps from our second-floor apartment to the reception area. Thankfully, Laura, our hostess at Santa Maria, has arrived. Giving clear directions, she recommends that we drive to the clinic in Montaione, about twenty-five minutes away.

Still in my nightie and housecoat, I stagger down the twenty steps, with Gordon's protective arm near but not around me. I cannot stand him touching me, the pain exaggerating every pressure point, every sound, every touch.

And I cannot sit in the car. Instead, I try to prop myself on my side, letting the seat belt contain me in the seat.

Yesterday's charming hilly country roads become torturous. Each bump agonizing. Each corner another assault on my body. Each hill a challenge.

We arrive at the clinic. Gordon leaves me to find the way to the proper reception. It takes forever, but when he returns he brings the doctor.

"Oy yoy!" exclaims the doctor as he sees my agony.

I limp to the examining room and immediately kneel on the cold floor with my face on a chair. He'll have to examine me from here.

And then I make a mistake. One that almost costs me my life. I forget that virtually no English is spoken in rural Italy. So when someone asks a question in English, it is important to assess the person's English proficiency. If it is low, the first answer will be the only answer—there will be no room for clarification.

"Have you had diarrhea?" the doctor asks.

"*Sì. Due,*" I respond.

"Aha! Here's a prescription for the diarrhea. You'll feel better by tomorrow."

No room for clarification that diarrhea wasn't the problem.

"Why are you kneeling?" he asks.

"There is something wrong down there."

"Aha! Here is a prescription for hemorrhoid cream."

"Hemorrhoids—*no!*"

"Let me see." He doesn't look as far as my anus but sees an inactive hemorrhoid, confirming his diagnosis.

As we settle back into the car and go searching for the pharmacy, I say to Gordon, "You know that I had traveller's diarrhea in Mexico. This is different. His diagnosis is wrong, but I'll take the pills."

Circling the town, Gordon eventually finds the pharmacy. The shards of pain are rising, and they are increasingly hot and corrosive. I wonder if I can make the trip back to the apartment. I do.

Stumbling up the stairs, I retreat to the support of that sturdy corner in the living room, giving strength to my legs. I manage to take the two pills and apply the cream. And wait.

I notice that my teeth are chattering uncontrollably. My fingers mimic the chattering of my teeth. Sweat is pouring from me. My heart is pounding, and I think that I am lucky to have such a strong heart. Mucus streams from my nostrils and pools on the floor; I have no energy to wipe it from my face. My entire abdomen is now under attack—filled with both pain and some kind of toxic aftermath. I try to hide all this from Gordon, but I'm pretty sure he is aware.

"I could die."

The thought comes, and when it arrives, I realize I have no fear of death. I have lived a full and complete life.

But dying can be painful. I ask Gordon to get an ambulance.

Again, he rushes down those twenty steps, and to my relief, he is back almost immediately. An ambulance is on its way—it will be forty-five minutes or so. We wait together in silence. Each new pain sends me further away. Each new pain jolts Gordon with the agony of watching but not being able to help.

I remove my jewellery—my rings and earrings and watch—leaving it all on the bedside table. Hospitals prefer that patients bring no valuables.

Finally, the ambulance arrives—but without equipment to bring me down the twenty steps. I ask Gordon to remove my slippers and I walk down barefoot, relying on the wisdom of my bare feet to gain purchase on the terra cotta tile. Somehow, I climb the two steep metal steps into the ambulance and then onto a hard, cold metal bed shaped like a butcher's sink but without the drain. I'm told to lie on my back, and then the attendants strap me down. Agony.

My nightie and housecoat are now completely soaked with my sweat. I begin to shiver. There's no blanket on board, but the attendant removes his jacket and gently lays it over me before attaching me to the blood pressure cuff, heart monitor, and finger clip that measures oxygen. He turns to his communication responsibilities, informing the ER of my condition. I escape my bindings and lie on my side, writhing with each new pain and absorbing each bump as I slide back and forth, following the course of the steep and winding road, crossing from one side of a mountain to the other.

Gordon is following the ambulance in our car. I hope he can keep up. We're going fast. And how is he ever going to be able to find his way back to the apartment? It doesn't seem like there is a direct route to this hospital.

Within an hour, we are at the hospital in the city of Empoli. It is around 4:00 p.m.

The doctors are waiting. Dr. Lollio and Dr. Bing. Between them, they have good command of English.

After I'm transferred to a stretcher, and doubled over on my knees, Dr. Bing leans down and explains to me in her deep, soft voice, very firmly, very clearly, "You need to describe from the beginning, everything. It is very important for our diagnosis. We need to know everything."

Gasping under the barrage of yet more pain, so near to my heart now, I answer her questions.

"What have you eaten today?" Two cups of tea.

"Are you sure that is all?" There was milk in the tea.

"In the past twenty-four hours did you eat any fish?" No.

"Are you sure?" Yes.

"What did you eat in the past twenty-four hours?" For breakfast, fresh bread and a croissant, jam, fruit, and coffee. For lunch, at a vineyard, a wine tasting paired with Italian cuisine—small salad, meat and cheese, fresh bread, lasagna, and for dessert, something sweet. Cookies, I think. For supper, a spinach-and-fresh-cheese pizza at a trattoria in Alberi, near our apartment. And wine, of course.

"How did you feel yesterday?" On top of the world.

"*Scusami*?" I felt very good.

"How did you feel this morning?" Wonderful.

"No pain?" No pain. I was ready to be a tourist.

"When did the pain start?" At 8:00 a.m.—maybe a little before or after.

"What happened?"

And so I tell the whole story. Dr. Bing carefully notes each word, but I notice that three things stand out to her: the original pain occurred in the lower gut and it was without warning; the pain continued to build and fill my entire abdomen; and there was no diarrhea other than the two short bursts.

As she probes for more information, one of her hands calmly, lovingly, strokes my arm, easing the pain of talking, reassuring me that help is present. She tells me that she'll now arrange for diagnostic tests, and disappears.

Immediately, the nurses begin the task of removing my nightie and housecoat, now completely interlaced with my near-catatonic body. Sharp surgical scissors gently reduce my nightclothes to fabric shards: longer ones down my fully exposed back; tiny ones around my front, where the fabric is tightly pancaked between my torso, legs, and arms. When I'm finally naked, they wrap me in warm blankets—fetal comfort. A shot. Blessed relief from pain.

Gordon arrives at the hospital within a half hour of the ambulance.

"I didn't have the luxury of racing through the dozens of speeding checkpoints in the little towns along the way!" he exclaims.

We have a moment together. It is an effort to speak.

"If I die, know that I love you and that I want you to be happy."

"I know, and know that I love you." But Gordon's eyes are telling me something else: "You are not going to die."

Dr. Bing and Dr. Lollio arrive, looking grim. Dr. Bing does most of the talking; she seems more confident with English.

"The ultrasound and the X-ray indicate a perforated bowel. We will need to remove part of your colon—that is your lower bowel—and connect the parts. If we can, we'll do laparoscopic surgery, but there is a good chance we'll have to make a full incision in the abdomen. To allow the colon repair to heal, we will interrupt the flow of the bowel contents by putting in a temporary ileostomy. That part is pretty straightforward. We just open up the ileum and pull it to the outside of your stomach, where it gets attached to a collection bag."

Immediately, Gordon looks at me with concern. He knows that I have vowed that I would choose to die rather than have a colostomy bag. My mother had colon cancer and I watched her shrivel into herself, becoming fixated on the bag, its contents, and her cleanliness. She may have lived another ten years, but I lost my mother on the day of her surgery.

I'm not sure what the difference is between a colostomy bag and an ileostomy bag, but I guess that since the ileum is the part of the gut closer to the stomach, the contents of the bag will be more liquid. The colon is where the bowel contents are concentrated into more solid mass. But I am reassured by the quiet competence of Dr. Lollio and Dr. Bing. I believe them—that only a temporary bag will be needed. It's the word "temporary" that makes up my mind.

"If I have to have a bag, I will."

"Are you sure?" asks Gordon.

"Yes."

At some point, I see the ultrasound images—my abdomen is filled with what looks like pieces of algae, hanging on every organ. And my bowel looks like it has been attacked by shards of glass. I've never heard of an "in-body" experience, but I think I might have been having one. The images confirm what I have been visualizing all day—corrosive green gunk has invaded my inner cavity.

Reality shifts. Can it be that I have been at the hospital for less than an hour? We have entered a reality where every second is an hour, every hour a day. We must learn to live in the moment.

A nurse comes to check on me and tells us that nothing can happen until the blood work results are back. I wait. Gordon waits. One hour, two hours, *a lifetime*.

Surgery starts at 8:00 p.m., but I'm no longer present in my body.

I've escaped on a pursuit of finding loved ones who have died. Seeing a glow, I stop to watch. I go further and further toward that heavenly deep purple light. A curtain is lifting. Behind it lies the most beautiful place I've ever seen. A place of warm, pulsating, glowing, silvery-golden white light. A place of glorious peace and wholeness and silence. A place I long to be.

From my childhood, I hear my father's resonant voice filling the church at the end of evensong, as he gave the final benediction, "May the Peace that passeth all understanding be with you now and forevermore. Amen."

I am experiencing that peace, right now.

Although I instinctively know I am welcome, I don't approach the light. Instead, I draw in the love that is enfolding me from several "ones who have gone before." Their backs are toward me. They are filled with that same warm, pulsating white light.

One turns his head fully toward me, without moving the rest of his body. It is Philip. His right hand is raised. He moves his index finger side to side—just once.

And he fills me with knowledge, for there is no spoken language in this place, only shared comprehension: "Now is not your time. You have a choice. You don't have to be here. I ask that you choose to live, and take a message to Marnie. Tell her that it *was* my time. I had no choice. Tell her that I love her and have always loved her. And tell her that I will always be with her. Help her understand what you see here, and how it is possible for me to be with her, always."

Philip knows me well. When someone asks me for help, if I can, I do. Sadly, reluctantly, I turn away from that place of wonder and return to my ravaged body.

At 11:30 p.m., Dr. Lollio informs Gordon that I am out of surgery and that it is now a matter of waiting.

"As Dr. Bing and I diagnosed, your wife's bowel was perforated. We tried laparoscopic surgery, but it was not possible. We opened her abdominal wall—an incision from her breastbone to her pubic bone. The toxic contents of the bowel had filled her abdominal cavity. We washed it all out. We removed the perforated portion of her bowel and put in a temporary ileostomy to allow the bowel to heal.

"All being well, your wife will be in intensive care for a day or so and then discharged to the surgical ward. Visiting hours in intensive care are very limited, but we will make an exception for you tomorrow morning at nine."

The waiting for today is over. Gordon walks to the empty parking lot and tries to find his way to our apartment over the unfamiliar back roads of Tuscany, with only the light of the moon to guide him. A few wrong turns and an hour later, he stumbles up the twenty tile steps and is greeted by silence and the knowledge that he needs to communicate with our daughters, Michelle and Susan. A long day becomes longer as he tries to sort out what to say, and how to say it. He closes his email by saying, "If you say prayers, let them be for your mom tonight."

Sometime in the night, not long after the surgery, I awaken. Standing around me are Dr. Lollio and two nurses, along with several others.

"Do you have pain?" asks Dr. Lollio.

"No," I reply.

"Are you sure?"

"Yes."

It isn't pain I feel but complete exhaustion.

One of the nurses gently lifts my hands to her face and says her name: "Serena." I see her and nod. As I examine her face, I wonder if she is an angel, she is so beautiful. Her slightly oval face is framed by smooth dark eyebrows and straight dark hair in a short elfin style, exposing her perfectly shaped ears, neck, and head. Her eyes are large, round, the colour of dark chocolate. Her lips have just a hint of colour, as does her lightly tanned skin. But it is her countenance that captures my attention. A countenance of warmth and caring, bespeaking the person she is—someone to trust.

I point to the plastic mask I'm wearing to indicate that it is uncomfortable. I'm told I must wear it. It's an oxygen mask, but I can't understand why it hurts inside my nose and down my throat. They feel raw. "Maybe it's still the aftermath of vomiting," I think.

I drift off into a post-anaesthetic sleep.

When I awaken, I notice a clock hanging from the ceiling; it reads 2:35. Hospitals often use twenty-four-hour clocks, to avoid confusion between a.m. and p.m., so I assume it is nighttime. But I'm wide awake.

Looking from side to side, I discover I'm in a cavernous room of fifteen beds, spaced at least eight feet apart, with another four feet at the foot of the beds and much more at the head of the beds. There are curtain rods around each bed, with privacy curtains available but tossed over the rods, so the entire space is open.

With my peripheral vision, I can see all but the space immediately behind me.

Directly across from me is an open door leading to a long room. There is a large rectangular counter in the middle of the room with drawers at the end and a series of trash cans lined up across the front of the counter. Behind the counter are floor-to-ceiling cupboards that extend along the full length of the room. The doors of the cupboards are labelled. One door is open; inside are drawers, each labelled, each containing different drugs. This must be the pharmacy.

Also directly across from me, but just to the left, is a staff station with enough space to accommodate five or six nurses and doctors and their laptops. There is a pony wall surrounding three sides, hiding what is on the desk from general view. In front of this desk area are several beautifully crafted trollies finished in a soft yellow laminate and equipped with nursing supplies. Nothing out of place, everything at hand for efficient access for patient care. Behind the desk is another long room with an equally long table. The wall between the desk area and this room is glass, with a glass door that opens and closes silently. I guess it is some kind of staff common room.

At the far ends of the ward, to the left and to the right, are huge double doors. There are no tiles, but there are plenty of hard surfaces. The spotless floor is an industrial-grade poured flooring, gleaming white with turquoise spots scattered across its surface. The cabinetry, also turquoise, is Italian industrial grade, the likes of which one sees in fine cooking magazines and upscale kitchen design shops. The walls are covered to the tops of the eight-foot doors with scrubbable wall covering, and from there to the ceiling with another four feet of gleaming white paint. The ceiling is a suspended stainless-steel grid, housing ventilation as well as myriad lights and speakers that are an intimate part of hospital life.

From activity that comes later, I deduce that the space behind my bed is quite deep, allowing several caregivers to congregate. I learn suction is available for those who require it. For me, there is oxygen. And multiple carousels of drugs dripping through tubes and into my body.

There isn't much activity on the ward at this hour. Several beds down, two nurses are changing a dressing on a patient; I can't tell if it is a man or a woman. Next to me, another nurse gently rubs something onto the feet of a young man, then puts socks on him, and tents the sheet over a metal frame, keeping the weight of the sheet off his feet. At the long desk there are two people looking at their laptops and making notes. There's no one else around. It is quiet.

The time passes agonizingly slowly. Sleep is not an option, though I doze from time to time. To paraphrase Pooh in the book *The Tao of Pooh*, "I am." I am fully present in the here and now, but I am not part of it—I have no interaction with it. I am immobile, weak, unable even to sustain myself with my own oxygen intake. I become a part of all that is around me.

This is my home now.

2

5:00. FROM somewhere to my right, at the end of the ward, staff begin to appear—some stretching and yawning, some scratching their bellies, some smoothing their hair and rubbing their eyes, all seeking their first coffee of the day. Somewhere, there must be sleeping quarters for staff.

The first person up goes into the staff common room. Stretching, he takes a huge Italian coffee maker—the metal kind shaped like an hourglass that operates as a steam infuser—and fills it with water and coffee. Before long, the delicious aroma of fresh coffee fills the otherwise medicinal air of the ward. This is the signal. Staff stream into the room and then come out again, each with tiny paper cups of hot coffee they are swirling to dissolve the sugar. One gulp and the cups are thrown into the paper-recycling bins.

Another person goes into the same room and from a hidden space comes the sound of a spoon stirring a pot.

Meanwhile, the rest of the staff begin their morning routine—checking in on their patients. I'm part of it.

"Are you in pain?" comes the question, again.

No, I reply and am greeted with a relieved smile from Serena. But as she checks my blood pressure readouts, then my pulse, then my temperature, the relief on her face is replaced by concern. At the desk she confers with a doctor, who makes a phone call. Within minutes, someone wheels in a big cart and takes blood from my arm. Another cart arrives at my bed, and an ultrasound is performed on my abdomen. A third cart bears an electrocardiograph. Electrodes are attached to my body, and I can hear the beeping sound of my heart. Now I know why there is so much space around the beds—to allow for equipment to come to the patient.

Serena leans over me, stroking my forehead, and whispers something that I don't understand. Still, I am comforted simply by her gesture. She stays by my bedside until she's called to the long room. Everyone else is eating breakfast—some kind of porridge, I assume. And everyone is talking, all at the same time. The volume increases with the sound of each spoon hitting the bowl. I can't understand what they're saying, but judging by the laughter and the body language, there is a lot of friendly bantering and teasing going on—a sign of colleagues working together in an intense environment.

6:00. Dr. Lollio arrives. Does he ever sleep? And how can Italian men look so impossibly sexy when they are so unkempt—rough whiskers, rumpled pants, shirts half tucked in, sleepy eyes. He confers with Serena and the doctor on duty. They all look at the computer, then over at me, then back at the computer. I realize things aren't what they should be. Another nurse comes to take my temperature. She shows me the digital readout (which I can't see because I'm not wearing my glasses) and shakes her head with a soft "tsk

tsk," calling the result over to the three of them behind the desk. They call the reading back to her, to confirm. She yells her confirmation to them.

Dr. Lollio makes his decision and writes an order. Serena goes to the pharmacy and begins to open doors. From the drawers, she pulls out glass bottle after glass bottle after glass bottle of medications, slamming them loudly on the granite countertop. A colleague checks her selection against the doctor's order, dropping the bottles into a metal basket. Serena walks behind my bed and sets up another carousel with the additional drugs and attaches them to a tube connected to a port in my neck that I hadn't noticed.

"Now what?" I wonder. I want to see Gordon. I wish he were here, right now, to reassure me. But he isn't, and there's no one around who speaks English.

I have no choice. I go back to that zone of "I am."

From this neutral observation zone, I absorb the patterns on the ward. For each patient there is a nurse, dressed in well-fitting white pants and top. On the back of each top is a rectangular patch. I speculate that on the skin side of the patch is the name of the owner. For every two to three patients there is a doctor, dressed in similar garb but also wearing a white lab coat. Orderlies wear green. Although there are several different kinds of shoes, the most popular type is an industrial-grade clog in red, green, blue, black, pink—colours to match jewellery, watches, mood; who knows?

The noise level that began at breakfast continues to increase as nurses and the pharmacist prepare meds for their patients. Each glass bottle pulled out of the drawers is slammed onto the granite counter. For some, the contents are emptied into syringes, and then the glass bottles are thrown into special trash cans—as far as I can tell, there are three of them. CRASH... CRASH... CRASH. There seems to be a competition to make the most noise with the breaking glass.

And above the noise are their voices as they continue their conversations, not only with the person next to them but also with people at both ends of the room. As they walk out of the pharmacy, the conversations continue across the patients, from one end of the sixty-to-seventy-foot room to the other.

Empty med bottles are removed from carousels. CRASH... CRASH... CRASH as the bottles are thrown into more trash cans between each pair of beds. The louder the better, apparently.

I observe that as the noise level increases, so does the efficiency of the nurses (the orderlies—all male—don't seem to do much except make lewd remarks). The louder it is, the more focussed the nurses are. I'm learning that a hospital in Italy is different in more ways than language.

Then I notice another sound. Telephones. Dozens of telephones, each with its own ring. How could I have missed this? It seems to be a chaotic cacophony of sound—with no order. But I am wrong.

Each doctor and the head nurse have a hospital phone with similar formal, officious ring tones. Other phones are direct lines to hospital departments—like the one Serena used to call the lab to take my blood. They have a ring tone similar to an ambulance siren.

All of the staff have their own personal cellphones with rings ranging from the sublime to the ridiculous. All brilliant colours, some patterned with cartoon characters or elegant designs, some with flashing lights as well as ringers. Most phones are left on the desk at the staff station. They vibrate on the hard surface when ringing/singing/ticking/cracking, adding a whole new layer of sound.

One doctor has three personal phones, each in specially designed pockets in his hospital garb. I wonder, if they ever all ring at the same time, which one does he answer first—his bookie? His mistress? His wife?

Some rings demand immediate attention from a specific person. Some rings demand immediate attention from anyone who chooses to answer. Some rings are ignored but continue for minutes at a time.

For each call answered, there is a loud conversation that is layered onto the rest of the noise in the ward. For each call answered, if the call is for someone else, the name is yelled out across the room: "*Renaldo*" or "*Bernacia*" or "*Maria*." Equally loudly, the person replies, asking who is on the phone and what is needed. This exchange, loud enough to rival the sound of old-fashioned megaphones, continues until the person being called either comes to the phone or asks that a message be taken. After each call, everyone wants to know what the call was about—the report must be loud enough for everyone to hear, or else there is ribald teasing and speculation that continues until another topic piques their curiosity. All this happens in rapid-fire Italian, of course.

7:45. Shift change.

New people in street clothes appear and disappear into a room I hadn't noticed. When they reappear, they are wearing hospital uniforms. The ward empties of staff. They're all in the staff common room. There must be thirty-five or forty people in there, some sitting, some standing. "Communicating patient information," I think. But the head nurse appears to be holding a sheet of music. "What is this?" I wonder. Then I hear her singing. And with great gusto, a choir joins her. Music—a piece from *The Marriage of Figaro*, I think. What a wonderful way to introduce a shift change.

The staff stream out, chattering. Those going off shift clatter through all the phones on the desk to find their own. Serena forgets and has to come back for hers. Those coming on shift drop their phones in favourite places all over the ward.

I notice someone dressed differently than the rest. He seems a bit unusual, dressed in surgical blues, wearing an ineffective blue operating cap, black curly hair escaping from it, tumbling onto his shoulders and into his eyes. Soon it becomes apparent that he's responsible for the pharmacy. I call him "odd duck."

8:10. My new nurse is Maria. She and Rosa arrive with a basin of warm water. Unlooping the privacy curtains from the rods, they close them and then gently, gently wash away the sweat and mucus and tears and medical astringents from my body. Even more gently, they pat my skin dry. With damp hands, Maria tries to smooth my unruly hair. And carefully, Rosa sponges my mouth clean, trying to erase the taste of yesterday's vomit. All the while, there is a steady stream of Italian conversation between them, along with frequent loud remarks to others in the ward.

The next step is painful. My sheets are wet from the sponge bath and must be changed from under me, requiring them to roll me onto my side. Fresh tears wet my face as my incision screams out in rebellion.

The curtains are looped back over the rods, and I'm exposed to the ward once more. Maria and Rosa move to the young man next to me with a new set of supplies and repeat the whole process.

8:30. CRASH...CRASH...CRASH...CRASH...CRASH. The sound startles me from a doze. It comes from right behind me. Maria is replacing my now empty med bottles with fresh ones. I count. Yes, five bottles.

9:00. I doze off again, but when I open my eyes, Gordon is here—my rock. We look at each other with love and relief pouring from our eyes. There's time for a simple brush of his lips against my forehead, and then Dr. Lollio appears, looking grim. What he says gives us cause for concern.

"Overnight, peritonitis set in, bringing a high fever and causing your blood pressure to drop and elevating your white blood cell count. We have you on concentrated antibiotics to tackle the infection and also medication to raise your blood pressure. We'll be giving you something for pain. You'll be in intensive care until you are free of infection. We don't know for how long," he concludes.

The guck that had poured from my colon into my peritoneal cavity had been there for too long. It had done its damage, and now I am invaded by a new enemy—infection through the whole cavity, attacking my entire body.

While we're still trying to absorb the news, Maria storms in. Using a pantomime of gestures, supplemented by a stream of Italian, she informs Gordon that he must buy body wash, lotion, and a brush for me—the hospital does not provide personal care supplies. The contrast of the gentle Maria who had recently bathed me and this assertive Maria is jarring, yet her point is made. Gordon must wend his way through Empoli to find a store with these products—it's a new experience for him to buy such items for me, let alone do so in Italy with labels in Italian and Italian-speaking shopkeepers. Languages are not his strong suit.

Gordon has driven for an hour to see me, but after ten minutes, I am exhausted. I ask him to leave, but before he goes, I ask when he'll be back.

"Visiting hours are limited in the ICU," he replies. "I'll be here at 1:00 p.m. and then again at 6:00 p.m." He touches my cheek, but before he has turned to leave, I'm asleep. The infection and the drugs wage their battle.

10:52. CRASH... CRASH... CRASH. CRASH... CRASH... CRASH. CRASH... CRASH... CRASH.

The racket is deafening. I open my eyes to see cleaning staff taking trash cans from the pharmacy and from between the beds to somewhere out of sight. Dozens upon dozens of glass med bottles tumble onto one another, smashing into each other and the walls of a large receptacle. Over this din, the volume of the conversations increases to accommodate this new noise, the women's voices rising in pitch to near shrieks.

Then another noise. The sound of grinding. Does the glass really get ground into dust, right here in the hospital?

I try to remember what it is like in Canadian hospitals. Is it this noisy? Do we use glass for our medications? Then I catch a glimpse of the plastic bag attached to my catheter and remember my father's drug carousel, laden with plastic bladders filled with drugs. And I recall a conversation I had with a fellow passenger as we were boarding our plane in Vancouver. It was about the need to conserve petroleum, so that our really important uses—like manufacturing plastic products for the health care system—are sustainable. Yet here in a hospital in Italy, I have to look hard to see plastic. Hmmm. Italy is part of the European Union. Where is all this glass made? Is glass manufacturing and recycling part of their economic strategy? If all the hospitals in Europe use this much glass—that would contribute to a thriving industry!

Too much thinking. I fall asleep again but not for long. I learn that more important than sleep are hourly checks of my temperature. I hope I don't have to have hourly blood samples; my arm is still sore from the morning needle.

Food starts to arrive for those lucky enough to be able to eat. It smells good, but I have no appetite. My throat is so sore.

Once the patients are fed, the staff take turns eating lunch in the staff common room. Gradually, the room fills. The glass door is left open, allowing the conversation to storm into the ward. It is loud, repetitive, and argumentative. The subject? It sounds like what to have for dinner and who is going to pay.

"Why not?" I think. "While eating one meal, it is always important to plan the next!"

Eventually, the "odd duck" groans, throws up his hands, and surrenders. He'll be the one paying for lasagna tonight. He's reminded that they need salad and bread as well. He agrees and he's given a cheer. Everyone comes chattering out, rushing to the pharmacy to prepare refills for the patients' meds.

CRASH... CRASH... CRASH... tinkle, tinkle CRASH fills the air once more.

13:00. It's visiting hours and Gordon walks through the double doors to the left, triumphantly holding three items—a plastic hairbrush that looks like a pink hedgehog and two containers.

Maria comes bustling in, examines the containers, and through another pantomime conveys that he has brought two lotions but no body wash. *Sigh*. Gordon's shoulders sag. He has to return to the mall to make an exchange—another language challenge to overcome. He confides that he had a lovely non-verbal conversation with a woman who was shopping in the same aisle and was sure that she had understood what he needed. Guess not.

He asks which lotion I would like to keep. I really don't care, so I point to the smaller container.

Gordon tells me about his morning. He walked to the mall with Dr. Bing, who gave assurances that there had been no indication of cancer. She also said that my bowel seemed to be very strong, making the whole incident quite perplexing. He went to the hospital's finance department; they needed my health care card number and other personal information. Gordon wanted to make sure he was doing everything properly for our health insurance claim. And he found a pizza place for lunch.

Within ten minutes, it is clear that even listening is beyond my ability. He understands. He is so caring. I cannot believe how lucky I am to have him in my life. He gives me a brief touch with reassurance that he'll be back at six in the evening.

For the rest of the afternoon, I doze on and off. Real sleep is impossible. Every hour my temperature is taken. Every half hour the blood pressure cuff automatically activates, squeezing my arm painfully. Every three hours my meds are changed. And there is that incessant crashing of glass bottles, loud bantering, clamouring telephones with subsequent one-sided conversations. No peace. No quiet.

18:00. Gordon returns, with a different container. Maria rushes over, looks at it, nods her approval at the body wash, puts it with my other personal items somewhere behind me, and then disappears. Relieved, Gordon and I have quiet time together. Few words are spoken by either of us. We're just happy to be together. Once again, within minutes even quiet visiting is too much. We say good night. I receive a light touch of his lips on my forehead. He heads to the car for his hour-long drive back to our apartment, to prepare his evening meal and send messages home. His day is far from over.

Visiting hours aren't over, either. The parents of the youth in the bed next to me are still here, faces stoic, bodies rigid. They quietly speak in what sounds like Filipino. A young woman arrives—their daughter, it seems. The father leaves mother and daughter to be together.

For a while there is silence. Then suddenly there are racking sobs.

In English, the daughter cries out to her mother, "I never liked him until just a while ago. I thought he was so spoiled. I never allowed myself to get to know him. Now I never will."

Mother rocks daughter in her arms, allowing the grief to spill over the youth and echo out into the ward.

A buzzer announces the end of visiting hours. Several groups ignore it. The buzzer sounds again, more loudly. Eventually, the staff have to herd the people out of the ward, much to the annoyance of the visitors. But there's a reason for the firmness: after they get the patients ready for the night, it's dinnertime!

CRASH...CRASH...CRASH—this time the sounds are rapid-fire. The "odd duck" has placed the dinner order, and that is the topic of all the conversations. I can see the occasional drops of saliva flying and realize some are actually salivating at the thought of food.

A lighted buzzer over the double doors to the right announces the arrival of dinner. The final med bottles are discarded. Disposable blue surgical gloves are snapped off and thrown into recycling bins. There is an exodus to the common room. For a moment, there is silence as people help themselves to dinner and sit down to eat. After the first few bites, though, the conversation starts again, first quietly and then ever louder. The topic? The state of the Italian economy and the negative impact that Greece and Spain are having on Italy. I guess that there are several differing points of view— no one gets to finish their sentence before being challenged. Nothing like a good political discussion to aid digestion! Before they leave the room, a cheer is given for dinner.

CRASH!! The sound of glass breaking then splintering into smaller shards fills the room, echoing across the walls and floors, hard surfaces allowing the sound to expand.

Green...red...green...red—a strobe light casts its secret message in flickers. An ambulance siren invades the air just vacated by the sound of shattering glass. A telephone shrieks to be answered.

A cleaning attendant passes in front of me wearing blue scrubs and orange badges, leaving yellow caution signs behind to warn of a wet floor. The tile is now slippery and dangerous underfoot.

I re-enter my state of "I am" for hours. I'm not sleeping, but I'm not a part of the activity around me either, even when the night shift arrives. Perhaps Serena notices this, because she adds another bottle to my carousel of drugs. With all the drugs on the carousel, why would I notice one more?

I see the clock on the wall: 2:05.

Morpheus descends. Not with the sanguine face of bucolic dreams but as a dreadful dragon with two heads: orange-flamed, yellow-fanged Fear and slime-green, rotten-toothed Doubt.

Together, they attack! They attack my tender underbelly of Trust. Ripping into it with their snouts and disgusting mouths, they destroy my Trust instantly, playing games as they toss me, pulling at my catheters, drip lines, and tubes. Screaming at each other to play harder, to destroy me completely.

CRASH!! More glass breaks as they shriek with joy at the shards lying around me, reaching to grasp those shards and impale me. They untwine their necks, showing that they are joined just at their tail; their reach is enormous. Digging into my intestines with their filthy claws, stretching them from one end of the ward to the other, screeching with glee, they let go. *Snap!* My guts retract, spewing out their disgusting, stinking contents everywhere, all over the sparkling clean walls, trollies, beds—even the patients.

The double-headed monster stretches me out again, until there is no elasticity left, and then races through the ward, winding my innards on the curtain rods, a reminder that Morpheus and his legions are the destroyers.

"Lisbeth. Lisbeth."

Someone is holding my face, but Lisbeth isn't my name. I hear the voice again, a little more urgent this time.

"Lisbeth."

When I open my eyes, it is Serena, just inches away.

"Lisbeth. Lisbeth. Do you remember what happened?"

No.

"You had surgery. And you are still very ill."

Oh. I nod to let her know I understand. I long to ask her why she was calling me Lisbeth—maybe she misread my chart. Elizabeth is my middle name.

Then I see the clock again: 3:08. Now I know that I can trust no one. The clock is being manipulated, just like the rest of me. The dragon had me for hours, maybe even days, not just an hour or so. I see so many tubes and lines attached to me and can feel others under the covers. I am trapped—bound.

Morpheus descends again.

I am a prisoner in a war camp. I'm one of the lucky ones. The others are dissected alive, but they are testing me to find out how much drug experimentation I can withstand before being convinced to eat myself into shards of flesh. I'm naked beneath a harsh orange metallic blanket. The guard wears dark blue coveralls caked with the blood of others who have taken this desperate route. Thrashing about, I try to escape these lines and tubes before I succumb to the temptation of self-destruction.

Strong hands hold me down. Two sets of strong hands. I am put in restraints. And then there is a soft crooning as sweat is wiped from my face and my arm muscles are gently rubbed into relaxation. Serena tries to connect with me with her limited English. Becca, the strong one, connects with me by touch and intuition, all the while humming an Italian lullaby, singing my name, "Lisbeth," as part of the song, as mothers often do.

I determine how to avoid Morpheus: *Stay Awake*!

Time passes so slowly. The clock is digital. There is no second hand to watch. Could one minute really be so interminably long? I decide this is how I will stay awake. I'll observe what can be done in one minute.

I am amazed.

In one minute, a quietly moaning woman on a gurney can be pushed through the double doors to the right, taken to a bed, gently slid from the gurney to the bed using a slippery red board, and have the med bottles transferred from the gurney's carousel to the ICU carousel.

In one minute, my temperature can be taken, my blood pressure recorded, my urine bag emptied and replaced.

In one minute, a telephone call from another department can be answered, a bed prepared, and an ambulance arrive, delivering a patient directly to the ICU, bypassing Emergency. (This one baffles me—why would someone be admitted directly to the ICU?)

Can I do this much in one minute? If I ever leave the hospital, I'll find out.

The night passes, minute by minute. I am able to avoid Morpheus.

3

SEPTEMBER 23

5:00. THE morning routine begins—the shuffling of feet, the yawning, stretching, scratching of bellies, searching for coffee. And once the caffeine and sugar combination hits, the conversation volume increases until the crashing of glass med bottles simply adds depth to the noise rather than a distinct sound. Like cymbals in an orchestra, the sound of glass breaking is only distinct when there is relative silence—punctuation to the preceding sound. Today, that isn't happening; the sound of voices outstrips the sound of crashing glass.

Serena's wrinkled brow tells me that still my temperature is high and my blood pressure low. I don't know about my other vital signs.

7:45. Shift change is different today. The head nurse isn't around; there is no singing. I'm sad. I realize that Serena and Maria share the twenty-four-hour care I'm receiving. Two twelve-hour shifts. I wonder how many days in a row they work.

My sponge bath is as gentle and thorough as it was yesterday, but I smile to myself. Maria isn't using the body wash and lotion that Gordon brought. She's still using her own secret supply. Becca uses my new brush, though—trying to untangle my unruly mop of coarse, curly hair. Finally, she rubs water through it with her hands and slicks it down. It will only take moments for it to pop back into its unbrushed mess, but she'll discover that for herself.

Exhausted from the bath, I settle back into my state of "I am," absorbing everything around me without thought or judgment or movement.

The "odd duck" is back. Frequently, he wipes his nose with the backs of his hands. He sneezes into the air. He wears no surgical gloves. He wears no mask. He opens the drawers that contain medical supplies with his naked hands and crushes pills using his hands and a tool like a little rolling pin. He gathers the powder with his hands and puts it into a container, to be used on a patient by a nurse.

I see a blue trail of glittering germs snaking through the intensive care ward, the pharmacy, the staff common room, and across the staff station. I see nurses and doctors touching the same spots as the germs and notice where they go from there. Many of them go onto the disposable surgical gloves that are thrown away, but before that, they find their way to the patients on bandages and syringes and in medications. There are streams of germs spreading in all directions. I am a hidden camera, recording sanitary practices on the ward.

When patient baths and med replacements finish, the nurses begin a housekeeping routine that I didn't notice yesterday. But now I realize it did happen. First they top up the supplies on the trolleys and in the pharmacy. They empty the medical supply recycling bins. Then they sanitize all the flat surfaces in the ward as well as the vertical surfaces of the trolleys. The daily cleaning staff are responsible for washing the other vertical surfaces and the floors, as well as emptying the regular garbage bins.

No one sanitizes the phones. The streams of glittering blue germs don't take long to re-emerge.

Housekeeping produces new noises as bins are lifted then dropped, drawers are opened and slammed shut, boxes are collapsed by stomping feet, empty containers are thrown into bins with gusto. There is laughter, banter, and commentary from one person to another, some close by but many at opposite ends of the ward or even in different rooms. And of course the ringing of telephones never stops.

I notice something else that I must have missed yesterday. Over the course of the morning, staff come on shift while others leave. There isn't just one major staff change; there are other staggered shifts. This adds to the noise of greetings and farewells. Becca is one of them leaving.

Noise—a sign that the ICU is alive and well!

13:00 finally arrives, and so does Gordon. We barely have a chance to greet one another before Dr. Lollio arrives. He still looks grim.

"You are no worse, but no better," he says. "We have to continue the blood pressure medication, and of course the antibiotics to get the infection under control. We don't know how long it will take. If we think you need it, we'll give you pain medication as well."

We ask a few questions for clarification, but really, what more is there to know?

When we're left alone again, I try to tell Gordon about my hallucinations, but my throat is so sore and mouth so dry that I can barely talk. I give up.

Instead, Gordon tells me that the two couples from Florida whom we'd chatted with at the poolside on Thursday evening had spoken to him as they were leaving Santa Maria this morning. They expressed their regret that they hadn't been able to continue our conversation about Canada's health care system and learn more from us about our perceptions of the United States and the political situation there. But more than anything, they wanted to offer their concern for us, and their best wishes to me for a full and speedy recovery. Gordon was overwhelmed when one of the women, the one who had barely said a word during our poolside conversation, gave him a long, warm, caring hug before she left. He couldn't believe how much he had needed that hug, and how grateful he was for it. I silently bless the woman for her intuitive warmth. How I wish I could hug him.

After about fifteen minutes, I fade. Seeing this, Gordon says a gentle goodbye and leaves to find some lunch and a way to fill his afternoon before he returns for our evening visit. He makes for a lonely, worried, reluctant tourist.

With the visitors gone, the ward swings into action. Med bottles crash. Telephones ring. Bandages are changed. Sheets are straightened. And then there's an exodus to the staff room. Individual conversations become one universal conversation. Doors are banging in there. Drawers slamming, too. Through the glass window, I can see arms gesticulating to make a point. I comprehend. There is no food to make dinner. Great consternation. What to do? The "odd duck" is given another cheer for his contribution yesterday. All eyes turn to a doctor who wasn't on shift yesterday. After just a few hints, he generously offers to buy dinner—pizza. A great cheer greets his offer. He receives it with a smile, shakes his head, and walks back to the desk area to study his laptop.

This is a signal for everyone to return to work. Well, the nurses return to work. I have yet to observe the orderlies doing any serious work, other than contributing to the over-all noise level.

I retreat into myself, resting with eyes wide open, unwilling to succumb to sleep and the dangers that lie there. The afternoon passes oh so slowly. I will myself not to look at the clock more than once per hour, but the longest I last is fifteen minutes.

18:00 finally comes. Gordon arrives with stories to tell, so I ask him to raise the head of my bed in hopes that I won't fade out as quickly as I have been.

He tells me that while he was waiting to come in, he was sitting across from a mother and her adult daughter—"The ones visiting the young fellow in the bed next to you right now," he says. The daughter was quietly sobbing, trying to control herself but unable to. Gordon stood up, walked over to her, and motioned for her to stand. Perplexed but still sobbing, she did as he asked, and when he enveloped her in his arms, she fell against his shoulder. Gaining strength from him, she was able to gather her own strength and compose herself. When she turned away, she gave him a grateful look and was ready to be a support for her mother. Gordon doesn't know how important his act of kindness was—the poor mother has been bearing the sorrow of her son's illness as well as providing succour to her daughter. He has eased that burden, I'm sure.

He says that after leaving the hospital this afternoon, he decided to explore Tuscany a little, so he drove to Vinci, the birthplace of Leonardo da Vinci. On display there are his designs of cranes for lifting heavy objects and machines for making textiles. Gordon describes the little village set in olive groves and vineyards, all on a sloping hill, a perfect setting for the castle, Vinci's main feature. To his delight, he found a wonderful restaurant filled with local patrons and serving his favourite pasta—spaghetti with olive oil, garlic, and chilies, complemented with a green salad. All this and it was sunny and warm, too—"What Tuscany is all about," he says. I feel like I've shared the afternoon with him, his description is so complete.

Knowing that even listening is tiring for me, Gordon stops talking and allows silence to fall between us. It feels good. Not as good as lying in his arms at night before we fall asleep, but just having him beside me is comforting. I can feel his love surrounding me, and I need that, because I'm starting to get scared of falling asleep. He moves to the side of the bed, lowers it, then gently touches my cheek before leaving and says, "See you tomorrow at 1:00 p.m. Good night."

All hell breaks loose about an hour after the visitors leave. The staff are still eating their pizza when telephones start to ring, the buzzer screams, the strobe light shines its warning, and hospital staff from other departments stream in and out. Three empty ICU beds are rushed out into the hallway and return with patients in them. One patient has two broken legs and a broken arm. At the end of the ward, there's a separate room for this patient, one with supports suspended from the ceiling to elevate the arm and one leg. A small patient, maybe a child, is tucked around the corner, out of sight. The third patient is put in the empty bed beside me, and before long, I hear the sound of the nurse suctioning mucus at the first sound of congestion.

The evening cleaners arrive. The med bottles are dumped from their bins into the collection receptacle. The din becomes a roar, and if that isn't enough, the head doctor starts to clap his hands louder and louder, faster and faster, filling the ward with the harsh sound of bones rattling against one another, echoing in and around all of the other sounds. It is as if he wants to join in the chaos of sound, to be a part of it.

I don't notice the extra med bottle being added to my carousel of drugs. My eyes close.

Morpheus descends again.

I am being held hostage in a hospital by grey ghosts in ethereal blue gowns. Every major vein in my body—arms, legs, neck—has several ports, each with six openings, and each of these openings is connected to a drip line delivering drugs to my body. Hundreds of bottles surround me; they rattle as they deliver their contents to my disfigured body.

Catheters suction out my waste at a faster rate than I produce it, drying me from the inside. I struggle fitfully against all these invasions, fearful that the intent is to induce illness so that I can be held hostage longer and longer. I try to scream out my frustration, but there's an obstacle in my throat. I reach up to my face and tear that obstacle away. It is a mask—a grotesque translucent mask that is alive, breathing on its own. But there is still an obstacle in my throat. I tear at my face again and pull on a tube. I feel it move, but it is still in me. I pull some more, straining, stretching my arm. It's like a giant worm, resisting, wanting to stay inside of me, but I don't give up. It finally comes free—out from deep inside of me, through my nose. I look at it. Could that have been in me? It is so long. The obstacle is no longer in my throat, but now I cannot scream, or even murmur. And there is blood everywhere. "Good," I think. "Now I'll bleed to death and they won't be able to hold me hostage any longer."

Strong hands hold my shoulders down, but I free my right arm and deliver a blow to that grey ghost's face. I am released and I struggle to rip out the catheter. I am almost successful, but more strong arms stop me. I'm restrained once more, and Serena cups my face with her hands.

When I open my eyes, she asks, "Remember me?"

I nod.

Becca brings a laptop to my bed. She points to it. There are words there that she wants me to read. I can't see. I need my glasses. Serena understands and puts them on me. On the laptop is a sentence in Italian in the left-hand column and the English translation in the right-hand column. "What are you afraid of?" it reads.

I sigh. How can I describe the fears of a hallucination? But from somewhere comes the nub of my fear, so I write, "Who will pay for all this?"

Serena laughs softly and says, "In Italy, hospital is free."

But I know that doesn't apply to me. I'm a foreigner and can be charged whatever the powers-that-be want to charge. Her response has not eased my angst.

I can't see the clock tonight. The privacy curtains are closed around the youth next to me, so my sightline to the clock is blocked. Never mind. I resolve to stay awake and avoid Morpheus. It worked before; it will work again. I start by trying to explain to Serena that I had hallucinations . . . nightmares . . . bad dreams.

Eventually, she understands. She says one word: "morphine."

Serena stays by my bedside. My throat is sore, my mouth parched. It hurts to breathe. I ask without hope—"*Acqua?*"

She nods, moves behind me, and returns with a sponge-tipped syringe. She puts it to my mouth and from its broad tip comes a slow stream of water, moistening my mouth, and, when I am able to swallow, soothing my throat.

"*Grazie,*" I whisper hoarsely.

She strokes my hair and smiles her acknowledgement. These few drops of water are the first to pass my lips since this all happened—days ago.

Although Serena is there, and although I work hard to stay awake, I cannot fight off the effects of the drugs. The power of Morpheus is beyond me. Again and again, I'm drawn under, only to thrash fruitlessly against the restraints. Only to revisit the fear of being held against my will. Only to know that I will never again see Gordon, nor will I ever leave this hell where prison guards and ghostly figures impose their will against mine, and where double-headed dragons observe this new struggle with glee, waiting for their chance to attack. I cannot breathe. My heart pounds with my struggle and my fear. I must escape.

I leave my body in search of solace. The deep purple of the beyond is there to embrace me. I am alone but not afraid. This space is devoid of life, but it is not empty. It has an energy of its own, a spiritual energy that soothes.

I remain here for a long time, then notice a warm glow. It is Philip's energy, surrounded by the familiar energy of others I cannot identify. Philip's message is brief: "You promised me that you would choose to live. It is time to return." I am accompanied back to my body by this loving energy, but the energy does not come all the way with me. I feel abandoned.

Fear returns with a vengeance. I am alone. I am trapped. I cannot breathe. Something is suffocating me. *I must get it off!*

4

A DIFFERENT VOICE reaches out to me through my panic. It is not Serena; it is Maria.

"Lisbeth, Lisbeth," she croons, calling me back, urging me to open my eyes. When I do, the first thing I notice is the clock. It is 13:00. Visitors are with the other patients.

"Gordon?"

Maria points to the waiting area.

"Why isn't he here? Why won't you let him in?"

My fear returns like swallowed vomit threatening to erupt at any moment. Reality and hallucination intersect.

13:15. Gordon arrives. He is as distressed as I am. Being held back for fifteen minutes without explanation made him fear the worst. But I am alive! His relief is quickly replaced with consternation when it becomes clear to him that I am both confused and upset. Listening carefully to my garbled descriptions, and repeating them back to me, together we realize that the morphine Serena mentioned must be the cause of my distress.

The doctors arrive to update us on my condition, and before they get to say anything, Gordon gives clear direction: "No more morphine."

"But what if there is pain?" one asks.

I reply, "There won't be any pain."

The doctors apologize for not letting Gordon in promptly at 13:00. They wanted to make sure that I was calm enough for visitors. Last night, I not only pulled off the oxygen mask but also ripped the nasogastric tube completely out, causing quite a lot of bleeding. Now I understand why my throat had been bothering me so much—a nasogastric tube is very uncomfortable. But getting rid of it didn't help; in fact, my throat is even more sore, and I'm having trouble speaking. I wonder what damage I did to myself.

Then the doctors tell us the antibiotics are working. My blood pressure is returning to normal. But they don't take the blood pressure cuff off. I wish they would. Every time it activates, I feel like my arm is in a powerful vice. I long to get away from it. If my blood pressure is okay, why won't they take it off? I'm too exhausted to ask.

Shortly after the doctors leave, Gordon makes a motion to leave, too, but I ask him to stay. I need the comfort of his strength. He simply stands by my bed with his hands beside me, knowing that anything other than a fleeting touch is painful. Gradually, I relax. Seeing that I'm nearly asleep, he gently brushes my forehead and promises to be back at 6:00 p.m.

Light napping is all that is possible. Every half hour, the blood pressure cuff inflates until it feels like an iron manacle cutting off all my circulation. Blood samples must be taken from wherever they can find a vein near the surface—a challenge requiring several attempts, since my arms and legs are swollen from edema. The heart monitor must be hooked up for its daily record. The catheter must be checked. The catheter bag must be emptied, along with something else that requires attention on my abdomen, not to mention the incisions must be checked.

Each of these tasks is done separately, making real sleep impossible. With each interruption, I ask for "*acqua*." Sometimes there's a smile and a nod accompanied by the magical syringe filled with water. Sometimes the request is ignored or even responded to by a negative shake of the head. Each time water is given, a notation is made on my chart.

I notice that the "odd duck" has a full-blown cold and several other staff are now sniffling. But not Maria.

The noise is now a background sound—I've adjusted to it, though it is not a reassuring lullaby.

When the clock reads 17:45, I ask Maria to raise the head of my bed a bit and adjust the angle under my knees. I've been lying still and flat for days. Maybe that's why I struggle to stay alert during Gordon's visits. I am rewarded for my effort with a huge smile from Gordon when he comes. He is delighted to see even this small improvement.

He tells a charming story. While waiting to see me, he was playing a game on his iPad. The two little daughters of the woman he consoled yesterday leaned over his shoulder to see what he was doing. After he finished the game, he switched to mah-jong. Their eyes widened in recognition of the tiles. After watching him play for a minute or two, they realized he was seeking pairs of tiles. First one then the other would lean over and point to where they were. They had a lovely time, laughing together—a little happiness for them when their mother is so sad.

After fifteen minutes or so, I ask Gordon to return my bed to sleeping position. What seemed so simple when Maria did the adjustments requires instruction for the novice. A high-tech bed—everything moves with the touch of a button—is fodder for contortions! He gives me some water from the syringe before he leaves. His footsteps are a little lighter tonight. We had a nice visit.

I re-enter my state of "I am." I'm comfortable there.

The rule in the ICU is only two visitors at a time. But the youth next to me has many visitors tonight. Sombre. Silent. Stricken. Staff delay their dinner hour, letting the visitors stay as long as they wish. Not long after they leave, his heart monitor gives off the unmistakable sound of death. No effort is made to resuscitate. The doctor and nurse are gentle in their final examination, as are the rest of the staff when they come to take him away. So very respectful. I am filled with thankfulness for the caring professionalism of the staff.

Shift change brings Serena back to me but not Becca. I worry. Did I hit Becca last night? Is she all right? I don't know how to ask these questions through pantomime, so I have to let the worry go.

Shift change also brings someone new—an attractive young doctor. Before long, just from the intimate space I sense between them, I'm sure that Serena and he are sweet on each other. Delicious! A romance to watch.

I fall into a deep sleep only to be wakened by NEIGH... NEIGH... HEE-HAW... HEE-HAW. Where am I?

All heads are turned to the patient area just around the corner from me. NEIGH... NEIGH... HEE-HAW... HEE-HAW. The playful sound continues. The staff I can see are silent, as if they are holding their collective breath. And then I hear the soft wheezing chuckle of a tiny child, and a laboured *hee-haw*. As one, staff break into applause.

With smiles on their faces, they prepare meds for their patients. CRASH... CRASH... CRASH... tinkle, tinkle CRASH. The routine returns with cheerful banter, as if the child's response has been the result of all their efforts. I hear the sound of suctioning. Perhaps the horseplay sounds and the chuckle have relieved some congestion. From around the corner comes the new doctor; Serena gives him a very special smile of congratulation. He must be the child's doctor.

One by one, the patients settle. I'm the only one awake. I'm unwilling to succumb to Morpheus, even though I know there is no morphine drip tonight. I'm fearful. And quite rested from my earlier deep sleep.

Serena anxiously keeps watch. By 2:00, I'm still not asleep.

She asks, "Are you in pain?"

"No," I reply, "but I am dreaming of the time I can have tea."

I'm surprised when she replies, "You want tea? Oh, yes! You can," she says, leaving me but then returning to ask, "*Limone*?" No. "*Zucchero*?" No.

She looks at me with disbelief then turns away. Is she really going to bring some tea? She is gone a long time but returns with a paper cup and a straw.

"Not hot," she says, holding the cup for me.

I will never forget that first sip—light golden nectar fit for the gods. It is served clear and plain, and I savour its hints of lemon blossom honey. Refreshing. Soothing. I ease into the simple normality of tea.

"*Grazie*." I sigh in pleasure.

The rest of the night passes with its usual routine. There's no sleep for Serena or the child's nurse, but the rest of the staff emerge from their cocoons, shedding traces of sleep, making a beeline for the espresso pot and then returning to their duties. Once again, their first duty is changing the patients' meds. The noise escalates as the caffeine takes hold, and the rhythm is established with each crash of a glass bottle. From around the corner comes the sound of more horseplay. There's too much noise for me to know whether there is a response.

It's early yet for the symphony of phones, so when one does ring, there is a temporary lull until its caller is identified. Serena's doctor is called to answer. His voice is low, his body language still but strong. Whoever is on the other end would feel safe. When the call is finished, he lets everyone know that it was the child's mother and that he will allow her to come at nine. No one complains; they seem so pleased that there has been a change in the child's status.

Soon after shift change, Maria arrives with a pan of warm water. Yesterday I missed my sponge bath, thanks to the aftermath of my morphine dreams. She takes extra care today, washing the sweat of bad dreams away, even between my toes, drying me, then massaging my sore body with the lotion Gordon bought for me. She produces a sponge toothbrush, offering to rub my teeth and gums, but I ask to do it. I need to assert some independence. But just the simple task of cleaning my mouth tires me. When I ask for water, instead of giving me the syringe, she surprises me with a water-filled paper cup with a straw—perhaps a reward for my step toward independence?

From catching glimpses of my extremities during the sponge bath, I am shocked at how swollen I am. My feet and shins appear to be the size my thighs used to be, my thighs are enormous, my hands are so swollen that I cannot move my fingers, and there are no signs of veins at all, anywhere. I can't bend my head, so I have no view of my torso, but I can only surmise that it is equally swollen. This can't be good, yet I'm sure I've seen plenty of urine being collected through the catheter.

My assessment of swelling in the rest of my body is confirmed by Gordon when he arrives. He admits that he wasn't going to say anything, but since I mentioned it first, he tells me that my head and face are also very swollen. When the doctor comes, he tells us that the antibiotics are working, and they've taken me off the blood pressure meds. He even says that I might be moved to the surgical ward tomorrow.

As an aside, the doctor mentions that other symptoms I might be experiencing are linked to my forced inactivity. I decide he must be talking about the edema, so I resolve to do whatever exercises I can. Foot circles and hand movements are about all I can manage, but that's more than I've been doing. I start doing them right away. This makes Gordon grin. I can hear him thinking, "That's the woman I know! Determined."

As soon as visiting hours are over, I ask Maria for some tea.

With her eyebrows raised, she checks my chart. "Renaldo!... Renaldo!... Renaldo!!" she yells.

The laziest orderly of the bunch appears and takes her order: "Tea. Hot. *No limone. No zucchero.*"

He saunters away and comes back with afternoon tea—even cookies, which Maria snatches away before I can open the package. I reward Renaldo with a smile and a "*grazie.*" He seems surprised to be noticed.

While savouring my golden nectar, the commotion preceding a new patient starts. The officious ringing of interdepartmental phones. Lights flashing over the double doors to the right. Last-minute preparation of a patient bay. Bustling of the nurses (no orderlies appear) to transfer the patient from the ER bed to the ICU bed.

The new patient is my new neighbour, in the bed vacated by the youth who died. She is very old, and very still. As soon as she is settled, her doctor is there, reviewing her chart with the nurse. Each med bottle is checked against the chart and discussed. A blood pressure cuff is wrapped around her arm, and buttons are pushed on a machine, so I assume it will record her blood pressure automatically, just like mine. Also just like me, she is wearing electrode patches that are immediately hooked up to the electrocardiograph cart that arrived simultaneously with the patient. An oxygen mask is gently placed over her nose and mouth. In all these actions, there is no obvious haste, just pure efficiency.

And then the privacy curtains are pulled. My only source of information about the gravity of her condition is the hush in the room.

This doesn't last long. The imminent arrival of another patient is announced with all the usual racket, and the noise level returns to normal—perhaps elevated a bit, as if all that silence acted like a dam and the contained sounds must be released in a rush.

It is busy this afternoon. All the patients, except me, seem to need extra care. Suctioning is almost a continuous activity for at least three of the patients, maybe even the child around the corner as well. This ties up the nurses assigned to these patients, leaving the remaining nurses with the rest of the work—cleaning, refilling the medical supplies, checking vital signs, and replenishing meds for all of the patients, as well as responding to patients' requests for water, help with turning over, and answers to questions. Meanwhile, the incessantly ringing telephones and the banter while staff come and go add to the sense of urgency.

Lulled by the busyness, I am startled by the smell of food close to me. In front of me is a large bowl filled with yellow porridge. A tiny espresso-size spoon beside it makes the bowl seem even larger. I gather I'm supposed to eat. It looks like the glue my mother would serve for breakfast once in a while. But instead of it being the white of cream of wheat, it is the yellow of cornmeal. My throat constricts. I'm not sure I can swallow it any better than I could my mother's offering. But the nutritionist in me gives me a stern lecture: "If you want to heal, you need sustenance. Eat."

When I pick up the tiny spoon, I am stunned by the staff's insight. I am so weak that it would have been impossible for me to manage a spoon any larger. My hand is shaking, not from an uncontrollable urge to eat but from lack of strength and coordination. I poke the spoon into the gelatinous mass and pull out a small mouthful. It has more texture than cream of wheat but is just as tasteless. Somehow, I manage to swallow it, then put the spoon down and rest. The nutritionist returns in my head: "Decide how many more mouthfuls you can take, and then have that many."

Like a child, I decide to make it a game. I'll have as many mouthfuls as I can remember how to count in Italian. The first one is "*uno.*" Then, "*Due. Tre. Quattro. Cinque. Sei.*"

Maria comes by just as I congratulate myself for having had a mouthful for each number. She nudges my memory. "*Sette,*" she says.

I grimace and take one last mouthful. That's it. Even when she says, "*Otto,*" I'm done. She indicates that I've been eating semolina porridge, then offers me some tea to wash it down. That's a nice reward.

The routine on the ward is out of whack. My tea arrives at the same time as Gordon. Visiting hours coincide with the night shift's arrival. Between sips of tea and the escalating noise level, visiting is not easy. Plus, I see Becca at a distance. She has a bruise on her cheekbone. I worry. Did I do that to her?

I refocus on Gordon and we talk about what might need to be done back at the apartment—laundry and such. And I ask him to bring my eye mask to see if it helps me sleep, especially during the day. But it is clear that I'm fading fast.

Breathing is difficult and I feel so heavy. Laden. Like I'm sinking. Drowning. I'm relieved when Gordon leaves.

Becca comes to check on me right away, then scurries away to talk to a new doctor on shift. She returns and makes an adjustment behind me, then comes to my bedside. She adjusts my mask and tells me, "More oxygen." I *do* feel a little better right away.

Before she can leave, though, I grab her hand to get her attention. I reach up to her face and ask if I gave her the bruise.

"*No, no,*" she responds, but then she says something else in Italian that sounds like "It wasn't your fault." Her gentleness is soothing. I know that if I caused it, she has forgiven me. That doesn't make me feel any better. I tell her I am so sorry.

Gordon references my hand and foot exercises in his email update tonight. "She is such a determined fighter," he writes. "Don't ever get in her way or cross her, because this is the character she has. We all could use some of this characteristic." He also says, "A final note as to how she is . . . Before I left tonight, she started to give me some domestic instructions. A sure sign that she is back!"

23:00. The night has just begun for me. For the past two hours, I've been watching a new doctor search the Internet on his laptop, make copious handwritten notes, and then work on a document. I am very impressed that he is so engaged in his work. Research, perhaps? A medical paper? He calls Serena's beau over and talks to him, making frantic gestures in the air. Serena's beau comes over to me and in perfect English says, "The doctor is in love with your last name and has decided to write a fictional anthology on fishing, using your name as a pseudonym. He wonders if the author's first name should be Arthur or William."

I calmly reply: "Well, Ganong is actually my husband's last name, and since his grandfather was Arthur and his uncle was William, and they both loved to fish, either would be good choices. But William was a famous Canadian biologist and cartographer, so his name would fit historically."

Inside, of course, I'm not calm! If I had any stomach muscles at all, I would be chortling uncontrollably! Imagine. I thought he was working! And here he is composing fiction!

That isn't the end of it. Several hours later, the author/doctor slams his laptop shut and vociferously exudes frustration, his curly reddish hair bouncing as he shakes his head. If the document had been paper, it would have been torn to shreds then hurled in the air. Pacing up and down behind the desk, he waves his hands in the air and seems to be appealing to the gods for help. He looks over at me, bursts into a huge smile, marches over to his laptop, and begins again. Still asking for help from the gods, he looks up to the heavens and asks, "Michelangelo? *No... no... no.* Raphael? *No... no... no.* Ah! Ruben! *Sì... sì... sì!*" And his fingers move rapidly across the keyboard, while he mumbles, hums, and occasionally looks across at me with a serious expression.

A while later, Serena's beau sees my fascination with the activities of the author/doctor, whom I decide to call Dr. Lunatic. Curious himself, he goes over and asks about this recent effort. Nodding seriously as he receives the answer, he comes over to me. With twinkling eyes, he tells me, "The doctor sees you as a Rubenesque beauty in an opera of tragedy. He says the core aria for the opera will be completed by tomorrow morning. Perhaps you should try to sleep. You need your beauty rest!"

And now I remember that the author/doctor had insisted that I not leave the ICU tonight. Surely I'm not his muse. Surely that's not why he wanted me to stay. The sooner I get out of here, the better. This is all too close to the hallucinations I've had about being a captive.

5

SLEEP DOES come but so late that I sleep through the morning coffee shuffle and the early-morning shift change. When I wake, Serena's beau comes over and tells me that Serena had asked him to say goodbye for her. She has the next few days off, and when she comes back I won't be in the ICU.

"Thank you" seems such an insufficient expression when someone has cared for you during extreme illness, but this is all I have for him to take to her. He understands, and I know that she will hear my words from him. He cannot stay longer. It's time for the shift change meeting in the common room and the head nurse is back in charge.

Before the meeting starts, though, Dr. Lunatic produces pages of something, waving them in the air with grand flourishes. He closes the door and, holding his papers in front of him, appears to sing. I cannot hear a sound—the sirens begin again. The staff rush out. Dr. Lunatic has been upstaged by the drama of real life. Everyone turns to their morning routine.

Maria must be off for a few days, too. My new nurse is Federica. She reminds me of my friend Lorri back home. She has a perfectly shaped head, with pale blond hair only half an inch long all over—in perfectly even spikes. Rhinestone studs and gold hoops line the curves of both ears. Boisterous. Fun loving. A prankster. A joker. She speaks no English, but between us we quickly learn to communicate.

I tell her that we have been staying near Montaione. "Mon—tai—on—e!" she shrieks to everyone around—"Casa mia."

From that moment on, I am her best friend as well as her patient. If I thought my previous baths had been gentle perfection, I had no idea. My body lotion massage afterward is pure bliss. And because she is so strong, moving me to change my sheets offers no pain, just warm, dry sheets.

But as she is bathing me, worry builds in her eyes. When she is finished, she doesn't move on to bathe my neighbour but goes to the desk and picks up one of the hospital phones. For once, I can't hear what she is saying, but I know it is about me.

A young doctor arrives. A very quiet, very poised, very beautiful doctor, with long black hair tied in a severe knot at the nape of her neck, perfectly groomed black eyebrows, light olive skin, and deep blue eyes. She reviews my chart while Federica talks and then calmly examines me. Giving me a reassuring look, but no comment, she moves to the central desk and makes four phone calls. Does this mean I can't be transferred to the surgical ward today?

The X-ray cart arrives at my bedside. I must sit upright, without help, while the X-ray plate is set up behind me. My stomach muscles were severed by the incision during surgery. Sitting upright is agony for my back muscles, which have been dormant for days and now must support my entire body. I have no strength in my arms to offer any assistance by holding on to the bed rails. A few days ago, the X-ray had been taken by just slipping the plate under me. What is different now?

Another cart arrives. More blood is required, and still no elastic is used to raise my veins. The needle is poked into each of my arms without hitting a vein. Bruises immediately erupt from every attempt. The sheets are pulled down and a vein is found in my leg. It feels like pints of blood are taken from me, so many syringes are used.

Another cart comes. The ultrasound cart. I must lie first on one side and then on the other. Although Federica is strong, I must hold myself still—straining all of my muscles and stretching my incision painfully. The technician is aggressive and the procedure hurts. "Why do they need both an ultrasound and an X-ray?" I wonder. What is going on?

All the attention turns to a parade of doctors approaching from the left double doors—the same ones that Gordon comes through. Leading the parade is an ancient physician with a tanned balding head fringed by straight white hair hanging to his boney shoulders. The hair sways back and forth as he shuffles down the ward. He is wearing a white lab coat over a canary-yellow shirt and cardinal-red pants that reveal his ankles. Is this delegation for me?

They stop one bed short of mine. Their attention focusses on my neighbour—the old woman who hasn't stirred since she arrived. I can barely see her sheets move, though I can hear her oxygen mask working to keep her alive.

The ancient doctor holds out his hand. The ICU doctor charged with her care places her chart in gnarled fingers that cannot possibly hold such a thick file. But they do. Without glasses, he rapidly scans the information, reading so quickly it seems impossible that he is absorbing anything. He hands the file back, strokes his chin, and then rubs his eyebrow.

The other doctors shift on their feet and then lean forward as the ancient one delivers his assessment. One word: "*acqua.*" There is silence, and then from the delegation comes the release of a collective breath: "ahh."

They break into reverent discussion. It is quite apparent that the ancient one had sucked all of the information from the pages he had read, applied his experience and possibly his intuition, and had come up with a solution they had not considered. Eventually, there is agreement, and it is clear that they will be following his instructions. His work done, he turns on his blue-veined bare feet encased in elegant but scuffed brown loafers and exits, the delegation following behind. Who is he?

10:00. I guess there's no breakfast for me today. No tea, either.

The privacy curtains are closed around me. I'm left alone to drift.

My new doctor returns with a colleague, a rumpled physician with a grey pencil line of a moustache above his full lips. I notice his lips because when he speaks his voice is deep, low, serious, and extraordinarily calm. I am lulled by his voice as he converses with my doctor in Italian, until he utters three words in Latin that I understand and strike fear in my heart. "*Tertius gradus gangraena*": third-stage gangrene.

The two colleagues turn and leave. Will I ever get out of here?

Federica opens the curtains and loops them over the rods. They resemble my intestines from those hallucinations nights ago. The images return with a vengeance, stoking the fear instilled by the word "*gangraena.*"

All around me I see different staff—there must have been a major shift change. This team seems very familiar with one another—the noise level is greater than anything I have experienced and I see signs of sexual innuendo. Well, no, actually not innuendo—overt displays.

The young man over by the pharmacy completes a call. Everyone knows that he was speaking to his wife, who must have told him that she was ovulating. He moves his hips to demonstrate that he is going home for lunch to make babies. As he leaves, Federica calls out something that is apparently lewd—even the young man blushes. Federica screams with laughter. A nurse at the end of the ward calls out something to Federica, and the ribald bantering carries on with raucous laughter, accompanied by personal phone calls with ensuing loud conversations, shouted instructions, and always the sound of med bottles being smashed into shards of glass.

When the visitors arrive, the staff scurry to the staff room, where they calmly sit and eat, quietly chatting. Such a contrast!

Gordon arrives with a smile and a story. While waiting to come in, he offered empathy to the husband of the woman next to me. Gordon had been looking at our pictures from Paris and Florence on his iPad. The old man leaned over his shoulder and looked at them, too. He's a lovely old man, thin but perfectly erect, his face crevassed with criss-crossed lines, who is deeply worried about his wife of sixty years. From their non-verbal exchange, Gordon learned that he and his wife had lived in Florence and knew the places we had been in Paris. It was an unexpected moment of friendship shared by two strangers, deeply comforting for them both.

My new doctor arrives and tells me that I will probably be moving to the surgical ward today. Gordon and I look at each other and grin. I ask if I will get something to eat today. She shakes her head slowly but gives no explanation. I'm not really hungry. I hope I can have some tea, though.

Just as she is leaving, Gordon asks if she would write a prescription for him. He's realized that he doesn't have enough of his high blood pressure medication. He had packed enough for our vacation plus a week, but we'll be in Italy longer. She nods and Gordon gives her his pill bottle so that she can see exactly what he requires. She takes it over to the central desk and confers with another doctor. They agree on something and before long she brings back both the bottle and a prescription. Now all Gordon has to do is get the prescription filled at a pharmacy.

Before he leaves, he checks with the doctor to find out how he will find me if I am moved today. The doctor promises to be here and to lead him to me.

As the visitors exit the left double doors, from the right double doors enters a cleaning crew of three: two tiny men and one large woman, all wearing baggy blue coveralls. They bring with them buckets of foamy water and several ladders. Disappearing into the pharmacy, they set up their equipment and scour the walls; the ceiling; the cabinets, including the cabinet tops; the lighting, sound, and emergency fixtures attached to the ceiling; the doors; and the floors. Everything that hasn't been cleaned every day is cleaned today. I wonder if this is a weekly cleaning.

Within an hour, they vacate the pharmacy, just in time for the afternoon meds supply cycle. Then they attack the rest of the ward. The two men start at opposite ends and work toward the middle. They even scrub the tops of the curtain railings, and I see them removing the stainless-steel light fixture grids and cleaning inside the fixtures and then the grids themselves. My area will be the last to be cleaned.

The woman pulls everything out of the general washroom-cum-storage area—right into the ward where beds and trollies are wheeled. I realize that it will be a while before I can be moved; there is no room left. The pharmacy took only an hour for the three of them to clean, but the washroom is taking much longer. From what I can see, there are a lot of crevices, fixtures, and shelves to wash, and she cleans the sink and toilet several times before she is satisfied with the result. Finally, the floor is scrubbed and left to dry. Meanwhile, she tackles all the stuff she removed from the bathroom. If those trash cans and moveable storage carts had skin, they would be raw from her attention. I'm glad she's not the one to give me a sponge bath! But I sure understand why their coveralls are baggy—they need the ventilation. These people work hard!

They're still working when the sirens and phones start to go off. No one trips over the mess in the ward. No one even seems to notice. But it is clear that we are going to get some company in the ICU.

First, the man with broken limbs is brought out of his special room and trundled through the right double doors. The cleaning crew is directed to his vacated room and they scrub it down, finishing it just in time for the room to receive another patient.

A patient three beds down from me is moved. She has only been in the ICU for a day. Why can she be moved but not me?

Within moments of her vacated area being cleaned, a patient is brought in whose face and hands are completely bandaged. The privacy curtains are whipped into place. Two nurses and two doctors stay there for a long time. All I can hear is a heart monitor. For once, there is silence in the ward.

And then I wait.

Federica rummages around behind me. Eventually, she comes to me and asks me something. It takes me a while, but finally I understand that she wants to know where my nightie is. I pantomime that it was cut off of me in the ER. She wrinkles her forehead and then disappears. When she returns, she's carrying an operating room surgical gown and bringing my doctor to tell me that I'll have to wear it until my husband brings me a nightie. For the first time, I realize I've been naked for six days!

The doctor warns me that the surgical gown will be warm. She's right. It *is* very warm. I start to perspire immediately. And it is also scratchy. It is either new or it has been starched. Who cares? I'm being transferred to the surgical ward!

Now there's a lot of noise behind me as med bottles are dismantled from my bed poles and thrown away—crash, crash, crash... tinkle, tinkle... crash... crash as they slide into one another. Within seconds, the brakes on my bed are released and I'm being trundled around all the stuff still out on the floor. I go through those double doors on the right! On the other side, there is another bed and at least five new faces to greet me. The red slide board appears and I'm slid from one bed to the other.

One of the faces belongs to a woman with short dark hair with the beginnings of silver in it. She leans over and asks if I remember her. I don't.

"I'm Dr. Bing," she replies. "I operated on you."

How embarrassing. She was the doctor who was so kind while interviewing me when I first arrived in the ER. How could I forget? And then I realize that she had been wearing a surgical cap that day. I explain to her, and she smiles. Then she says, "I'm glad that you are recovering." Imagine.

Federica leans over and gives me a hug. She rubs my face tenderly with her hands, and then whispers, "*Bellissima.*" Her parting gift to me is to make me feel cherished.

Dr. Bing turns to the others and gives them some instructions in Italian that I don't catch. Two nurses hook up new meds, right there in the hallway. A strong-looking, square little woman all of five feet tall releases the brake and effortlessly pushes me toward the elevator. She leaves the rest rushing to catch up. Up three floors we go, to a sparkling clean hospital wing. Wide, silent hallways. We turn right and into my new home. A semi-private room. My space is beside a window. It is daylight, and I nearly weep—it has been so long since I've seen day or night.

Once I'm settled, I notice my roommate and her visitor, a young woman. I smile and introduce myself.

The young woman responds with a smile and says in perfect English, "Welcome. I am Sofia, and this is my mother, Anna."

When I comment on her English, she tells me that she works in the communications department of the hospital. Anna doesn't appear to speak English. I don't speak Italian. But I know we like each other, just by the way we communicate with our eyes. She doesn't know me, but we're both very proud mothers—we have that in common.

For a few moments, I enjoy the relative quiet of the room. There's just the murmur of conversation between Sofia and Anna, no sounds of breaking glass or ringing phones. Sofia leaves the room.

Then my doctor from the ICU arrives, with Gordon in tow. Having kept her promise to guide him to me, she leaves but is quickly replaced by the short, square woman. She is on a mission. She shouts instructions to Gordon. Unfortunately, the instructions are in Italian. Seeing she isn't understood, she shouts louder. Frustrated, she turns to Anna, asks her a question, and, receiving a nod of approval, opens a locker beside Anna's bed. She pulls out a long, wide elastic belt apparatus. She holds it out to Gordon and tries again with her instructions. Wow—she is getting exasperated with us both! Thankfully, Sofia returns and interprets. Gordon has to buy one of these things for me. *Right now.* What is it for? What size do I need? Where does he buy one?

We learn that now that I am out of the ICU, I'm expected to do as much as I can without help. Since my stomach muscles no longer work because of the incision, I need a support belt. *I'm to wear it all the time*—except when I'm lying down.

As for getting the right size, her look implies that we are really stupid. How could we not know what my size is? But she puts her hand in her pocket and pulls out a measuring tape. Sticking one hand under my back and raising me up agonizingly with the same motion, she takes a measurement, shows it to Gordon, and gives him an authoritative nod. He sheepishly nods back. (While she was bending over me, I noticed her name tag: Claudia.)

Somehow, we learn that there is a pharmacy nearby, and that's where he'll find these belts.

But we're not finished yet. She has another mission, and that's to tell Gordon that I'm *not* supposed to be wearing hospital clothes. She has to get that surgical gown back to the laundry, so I need a nightgown. *Right now.* It doesn't take much for me to realize what's going on—I had been told the same thing in the ICU (though not quite so emphatically)—so I'm able to be the interpreter for this exchange.

Gordon and I would love to have a little time together, but it is clear that Claudia will not leave until he obeys her orders. He gives up, indicates his compliance, and leaves. With a snort of triumph, Claudia exits right behind him. The room seems empty now, though Sofia and Anna are still here, quietly chatting for a bit. Eventually, Sofia says farewell to her mother.

Silence. No sound in the room. No sound from the corridor. How I love silence. How I have missed silence. I lie still, absorbing the peacefulness.

A chickadee lands on the window ledge outside my window. She perches, preens, and then roosts right there, for me to see. Of all birdlife, the chickadee is my favourite. And it seems one has adopted me.

I have no idea how long Gordon is gone. Maybe an hour, maybe two or three. When he arrives, he slips in unnoticed by me. He sits in the chair at the end of my bed, waiting for me to open my eyes and see what he has placed on the ledge, directly in my sight—a beautiful single long-stemmed rose.

It is exquisite. The expression on my face brings joy to his.

Claudia bustles in to see what he has purchased. She takes all the parcels from him and investigates each one, including Gordon's prescription, which he quickly grabs from her and desperately tries to explain is for him. To his relief, she believes him.

In one motion, she drops the packages on my bed, turns, whips the privacy curtains into place, and calls out, demanding assistance. She strips back the sheets and uses one hand to lift me again while untying the ties at the back of the surgical gown, before dropping me back onto the bed. I suddenly realize how sore I am, and how gentle the nurses have been in the ICU. Now naked except for the bandage down my midriff, I begin to shiver after having sweated for hours inside the hot hospital gown. Frustrated by the lack of response from her colleagues, Claudia yells out again for help, ignoring the call button on my bed. A large, very strong woman comes running in.

This time, one of them lifts my back, while the other shoves the support belt underneath me. Two sets of hands push my back into an arch and stretch to its limit the raw incision that runs from my sternum to my pubic bone, roughly rubbing their knuckles against my tender skin and bones. They get the belt in place, but it is upside down, so the procedure must be repeated. Finally, it is tightly wrapped around me and Velcroed together.

They sit me up in bed and put on my nightgown—the first one my husband has ever bought for me. It's pastel pink in a beautiful Italian cotton knit, with tiny tucks down the front, ivory lace, and long sleeves with lengthwise tucks forming the cuffs. It feels light, cool, reassuring. Soft. Feminine.

With a nod to me and the tiniest of smirks, Claudia marches out of the room. Gordon and I look at each other and chuckle. What else can we do?

I settle into my new sitting position in the bed, and Gordon recounts the full story of his recent shopping adventure.

As he left the hospital via the front door, he noticed a store across the road with a blue cross on the sign. It looked vaguely like the Red Cross insignia, so he thought it might have something to do with medical supplies. Sure enough, the tiny storefront was jammed floor to ceiling with all types of medical paraphernalia—but no obvious supply of support belts.

He asked his usual question: "Do you speak English?"

Having received a fairly common response, in words and with the universal hand and finger motion to signal "a little," he described what he needed. He was guided to an area where he was presented with an array of such belts, but none of the brand he'd been shown in the hospital. Fearing Claudia's stern reprisal if he made a mistake, he chose the best he could find and then had to pantomime the right size. Support belt in hand, he made his way to the cash register. And behold, stacked behind the cashier was a supply of the "right" brand. So he negotiated his way through returning his original choice to the stocked items and selecting another from the as-yet-unpriced merchandise.

But just as he was about to pay for the belt, something caught his eye at the back of the store. So he arranged to leave the belt with the cashier and headed to the back. The store was much deeper than it appeared, and there was a full pharmacy back there. So he approached the counter and presented his prescription. The next few seconds amazed him.

The pharmacist scanned the prescription and told Gordon to wait, but the pharmacist didn't move. Almost immediately, there was a small sound. The pharmacist turned around and picked up a dish containing exactly the right number of pills. The distribution of drugs in the pharmacy was fully automated! Looking again, Gordon could see a network of clear plastic tubes—the distribution system.

He was in for another surprise back at the cash register. He was expecting to pay a premium for his prescription; after all, he has no prescription coverage in Italy. But the cost was a fraction of what he would have paid in Canada, even after his prescription coverage. What an eye-opener!

In the middle of his story, afternoon tea arrives for me—in a cappuccino-size crockery cup that is far too heavy for me to lift. Eager for the delicate flavour, I shakily ladle it into my parched mouth with a tiny spoon, dripping spots of light amber liquid over the front of my new nightie.

Watching me savour my tea, Gordon continues with his story.

Having been given the assignment of finding a nightie, he decided to head back to the mall. There he realized that breakfast had been many hours ago. He'd noticed a food fair during another visit, so he checked out his options by looking at what people were eating. Spaghetti—plain with oil and garlic. Spaghetti—with plain tomato sauce. Spaghetti—and *fries*?

"Oh! Drool! Fries. Today that would be comfort food for me," Gordon thought.

Following his nose, he found the vendor—an entrepreneur with a barbecue pit, right in the middle of the mall! Specialty of the house? Beef. He ordered fries and a steak, medium. The steak turned out to be hamburger meat—fortunately, well done—but the flavours really did satisfy that need for comfort food, and he was prepared to pay the price of indigestion for the rest of the day. With a grin on his face, he tells me about it.

His next stop was a women's clothing store—a place he avoids as much as possible, but today there was no choice. Claudia had made herself clear. He couldn't return to the hospital without a nightie. He straightened his shoulders and walked into the store—a maze of racks, shelves, and tables, all laden with women's clothes. But nowhere obvious (that is, near the front door, the easy escape route) was there a nightie. So he had to ask for help, but this time in response to his question "Do you speak English?" there was a firm shake of the head ending with "No." So he pantomimed getting undressed, putting on a nightie, and getting into bed. (This scene is proof positive that he loves me!)

He tells me that he was prepared to lie down on the floor in a fetal position if it would have helped. Fortunately for him, this was unnecessary, as the sales clerk got the message. With a beckoning nod, she led him to the back of the store, first through an array of lingerie, then to a display of nighties. He had to dig through a multitude of silky see-through options to find a sedate hospital-suitable selection.

I had specifically asked for cotton, but he couldn't find what he classed as cotton, so he had to ask for more help. The sales clerk understood "cotton" and pointed out a pile of cotton knit nighties.

Perfect! But what size? The salesclerk was still there and was about my size. Between them, they were able to select one, and Gordon fled to the front to pay for his purchase.

On his way back to the hospital, his arms laden with purchases, he walked from a distant parking lot (free parking for hospital visitors!) along some back streets. And there he came across a flower shop. Flowers are something he has always taken great pleasure in bringing me. They never fail to bring a delighted smile to my face—a smile that he loves to see. He stepped into the doorway and found a beautiful dark-haired, dark-eyed woman smiling at the flower arrangement she was creating—the same kind of smile he was hoping to bring to my face.

The first flowers he had ever given me were red roses—a dozen—on Valentine's Day—twenty-eight years ago. Looking around in the display cooler he saw exactly what he wanted—a single long-stemmed red rose. Just a bud, ready to burst. The woman spoke English, which made his purchase easy. When he explained what had happened to me, she asked him to wait. Curious, he watched as she chose a small white vase, then wrapped the rose with a cloak of white tulle trimmed with satin. The tulle was shaped like a calla lily around the rose, accentuating its perfect beauty. Then she chose a beautiful piece of satin ribbon, the exact colour of the rose, and tied a perfect bow around the arrangement.

"So that was my shopping trip," he finishes, with a pleased smile on his face.

I touch my nightie and tell him that it is beautiful. And I nod to the red rose and bite my lip as tears spring to my eyes. His pleased smile gets wider, and our eyes hold each other for a long moment. Just the two of us.

I ask him to go shopping for one more thing.

"Now?" he asks.

"Yes, please, but you don't have to go far. Anna managed to explain to me that there is a vending machine in the visitors' area nearby, and that's where she gets her bottles of water. I can't lift the jug of water that the hospital provides."

Happily, he goes and brings back two bottles of water. Then he gives me a couple of euro coins so that if I need more, I can ask one of the staff to get it.

Gordon has had a long day. Also, he can see that I am tiring. Although it's early, we say good night and he begins his journey home to Santa Maria.

Anna is quiet. The hallways are quiet. I savour the peace, but now I can no longer ignore the feeling of heaviness throughout my body. My limbs are weighted down. My chest is full and heavy, making breathing difficult. Perspiration runs in rivers from my scalp down my neck, catching under my arms, thin rivulets dripping off the sides of my chest, making me shiver. I sink lower and lower into a deepening fatigue.

This time, the loving purple light is waiting for me nearby, enveloping me. I am swaddled among them—the faceless bearers of light and love. They enfold me, allowing me to stay with them for a while, but not forever. This time, they return with me and hover, comforting me. When they slowly fade away, I am awake, at peace.

I savour the quiet and Anna's companionable soft breathing as she sleeps.

Unbelievably, the chanting sound of a gospel choir begins, echoing through the corridor, softly, rhythmically. "Trust... in Him. He... is the light. He... is our saviour. *Sal-va-tion!*" Repeated over and over, until I am sure I am hallucinating again.

Over the sound of the chant comes a clear, strong voice. Male. British.

"Come, sinners. Jesus Christ is your salvation! You need His light to see the way. You are battling your sins. Your lust. Your greed. Your foolishness. Trust in Him. He will save you from your sins. He will help you. Happiness is here for you. All you must do is trust and accept. Come to me and I will help you find Him. Jesus Christ is your salvation!"

The choir repeats the message, ending with its chorus. "Trust... in Him. He... is the light. He... is our saviour. *Sal-va-tion!*"

Silence.

Have I imagined this? How could—why would—there be a gospel service in English, in a hospital here in Empoli, the heart of Tuscany?

Rapid footsteps. Leather-soled shoes slap the hard, slippery floor. Two coins drop into a pay phone. A male voice, with a heavy Italian accent but speaking English. The voice filled with longing.

"I must see you again. Last night ... you made me feel more like a man than ever before. I must see you ... When? Oh—yes, yes ... Oh ... But last night ... How much would it be ...? But all I want to do is to look at you ... I see ... Yes, yes—I'll see you then! We'll meet at the same table ...? Good!"

No movement.

Two more coins drop. A low, hurried conversation, with a loud, frantic ending.

"I don't know how you're going to get it for me, but I need it now. I must have the money now and no one must know!"

The phone crashes onto the hook.

A few hesitant footsteps, then an agonized cry: "Father, Father—help me!"

The leather-soled shoes beat a hurried path back down the corridor.

"Help me, Father."

Sobbing.

Two pairs of leather shoes return slowly, softly down the corridor, stopping not far from my room's doorway. There must be seats there, or an office. I hear the sounds of two people settling into chairs. The sobbing gradually subsides.

"What is it, my son?" enquires the same voice that I heard preaching such a short time ago. It is a gentle, calm voice now.

"Father, I have been tempted. I *am* so tempted. I fear for my life."

The conversation continues, but I can't hear it. The preacher's voice is soft but probing. The other man's voice is no more than a desperate, pleading whisper.

And then, the preacher's voice becomes strong and stern.

"Is it your life that you fear for, or that you can't have what you have in your life, and this, too . . .? This isn't something that you're just thinking about, is it . . .? You've already started to put it into motion, haven't you . . .? What are you going to do?"

"I . . . *won't go.*" The man sobs.

"Are you sure?"

"*Yes.*"

"If you need to talk to me, if you become weak, if you become tempted, you can call me—anytime. Do you understand?"

"Yes. Thank you, Father." And then a less brave, whispered, "*Thank you.*"

Two sets of footsteps travel in opposite directions, one set sure and steady, the other slow and shuffling.

Silence fills the hallway and my room.

I can hear Anna softly snoring, but I can't sleep. I'm afraid of letting go, the horrors of morphine-induced hallucinations still vivid in my mind. I promise myself that I'll ask for a sleeping aid for tomorrow night.

In the middle of the night, a nurse comes to check on me. The finger clip that tracks my oxygen level has slipped off (actually, it was starting to hurt, so I flicked it off). She replaces it, then waits to see the results on the machine by my bed. Within moments, she goes into action—calling someone, answering questions, gently removing the small nasal oxygen harness and replacing it with a full oxygen mask, and then fiddling with the dial for oxygen flow. She pantomimes that I must keep the mask on, pats my shoulder, and leaves. But she returns frequently, adjusting the mask and the dial.

6

———

AT DAWN, the chickadee and I greet each other through the glass. I hope there is food and water nearby. I would miss this tiny companion if she had to fly away for long.

There is no breakfast for me, just more blood samples, X-rays, and another ultrasound. Faces are grim. No reassuring smiles. No sponge bath. Not even any tea. Just the ever-ready stream of glass bottles filled with fluids being hooked up to me, and the oxygen mask strapped tightly to my face. I thought I was finished with all this. I'm so weak— no, really, I'm so tired—I don't even care.

On his way to my room, Gordon was stopped by Dr. Lollio, who explained that they must drain the fluid that has collected around my lungs. There is so much that it is interfering with my ability to breathe, and that is why I must wear the oxygen mask right now. My oxygen levels are dangerously low. He also told Gordon that as soon as this is done, I will feel better. We both think that sounds like good news. Then maybe I can start walking and regaining some strength.

Dr. Lollio told Gordon the procedure would happen very soon. In anticipation, Gordon decides to wait with me.

Lunchtime comes. Gordon leaves.

Refreshed from lunch, Gordon returns. With him by my side, I am able to relax and nap.

Late in the afternoon, there is a bustle of activity. Entering my room is Dr. Lollio, the doctor with the pencil-thin grey moustache over full lips, a young female intern with blond hair pulled into a ponytail, two nurses, a cart with strange-looking supplies, and another cart with some kind of portable machine on it.

Gordon and Anna are asked to leave the room. As Anna bounces out of the chair, I am struck by how nimble she is, even though she has to wear the same support belt I do. I'll have to ask Sofia how long Anna has been in the hospital. Maybe I'll be that agile soon.

Dr. Lollio apologizes to me for the delay. There had been a very serious accident and the doctor with the pencil moustache has been in the operating room for many hours. No wonder he looks so weary. Then he explains that the intern will be doing my procedure, under the supervision of the doctor. The procedure absolutely must be done today.

Why, oh why, did I need that information? I hope she has done the procedure before. I really don't want to be a guinea pig.

I'm told that I must sit up on the side of the bed, with my feet dangling over the edge. I look at them, thinking they have completely lost their minds. I can't even sit up by myself, let alone dangle my legs. The two nurses take care of that. Once I'm in position with my back to the intern, the doctor, and the carts, my beautiful pink nightgown is removed. One nurse stands in front of me, holding me. She is strong, and soft. Her name is Marta.

Two injections of local anaesthetic are to be given, one on either side of my spine. That is all the explanation I'm given for what is about to happen.

During the first injection, on my right side, the needle hits a bone. The pain is excruciating. Then, as the anaesthetic is released, I feel that I am being burned alive from the inside out. My moan has frightened the intern. She is loath to start the next phase—inserting tiny drainage tubes through the skin, between my ribs, and into my pleural sac. Her mentor calmly, softly coaches her (in Italian, thank heavens)—I imagine he's reminding her of all the training and experience she has received. His melodious, deep baritone voice soothes both the intern and me. Eventually, she begins.

I had expected the procedure to be as painless as acupuncture. How foolish. The pain is beyond belief. I can feel every jab of the tiny tubes, every millimetre of slow progress from insertion to drainage point, every turn, every adjustment to circumvent ribs, every prick of the pleural sac. What would it have been like without the anaesthetic?

One... two... *I feel faint*... three... four...

The nurse in front of me moves from supporting me to cradling me in her arms, stroking my hair as a mother would to soothe a child...

Five...

"*How many more?*" I sob.

"Just a few," replies the intern.

She is about to insert one more, and I hear the doctor say to her, "Not there. Remember the rule. Only the safe space between the lung and the liver." I guess that the machine on the cart is helping to provide a reference point as to where the insertions should go.

As the intern prepares to inject me on my left side, I cringe. The doctor takes the syringe and carefully and surely inserts the needle and releases the anaesthetic. Although it burns, no bone is hit and I'm saved that previous excruciating pain.

More insertions. After five, I lose count. By the end, I reek of foul perspiration and am dizzy from pain. The front of the nurse's uniform is soaked with my sweat and tears. I have collapsed in her arms—they must be aching from the support they have given me.

The doctor comes around to the other side of the bed to speak to me. "You will feel better now. Already a litre of fluid has been drained." He holds a bladder bag of yellowish fluid to show me. "We'll bandage these tubes in place so they can continue to drain. Then you can lie down and rest." He gives me a grave smile, his face even wearier than when he arrived.

True to his word, the tubes are patted into place and a bandage placed over my entire back; then my nightie is put back on.

Does the doctor really think I will be able to rest, lying on my back with all these tubes stuck in me? Now I know what an upside-down porcupine feels like! (A mutant porcupine with quills directed inwards.)

Gordon and Anna return. One look at them and a sob escapes me. Anna slips between our beds to close the curtains while Gordon quickly moves toward me. I want his arms wrapped around me, but I can't let him hold me—my back is just too tender. So he perches on the bed and holds my hand. This is good for a while, but eventually neither of us is comfortable. We agree that it is time to call it a day—after Gordon brings another bottle of water and loosens the lid for me.

Anna's husband comes for a visit. I can just see the doorway from around the curtain. Claudia and Sofia bring dinner trays for them, which is a good thing since they don't share any conversation. Once the clattering of cutlery on china ceases, I can hear the shifting of a newspaper. A cellphone blares out the first grand chords of Beethoven's Ninth: Da— Da—Da—DAA. No timid ring for diminutive Anna, I think, as I hear her answer with the typical Italian greeting: "*Pronto!*"

Hubby leaves. I get a glimpse of his fringed bald head, bent back, and bow-legged walk. He's about the same height as Anna but broader, and his gait is slower, even though Anna has had some serious surgery recently. I wonder how old they are.

There is an after-supper lull and I can see it is getting dark outside. My little chickadee is settled on the window ledge, head tucked in, chest puffed out, and wings wrapped around, trapping her warmth. We're both content just to be. Anna is looking through a *Vogue* magazine Sofia left. She's turning the pages slowly and quietly. She, too, seems content.

There's a gentle knocking at our open door. "Tante Anna?"

Anna welcomes a beautifully groomed woman, impeccably dressed, not a wrinkle to be seen on her clothes or her face, though she's probably in her late forties. A niece? A cousin? A friend? A hesitant question from the visitor leads to a lengthy and voluble response from Anna—I gather she's talking about her recent surgery. But that's it for Anna. It sounds like the visitor launches into a lecture about the curative powers of olive oil, referencing Saint Zopito and Loreto oil of the Abruzzo region. The monologue goes on and on. Anna is stoic throughout, shrugs her shoulders, and, when given a chance, starts to respond. I hold my breath, hoping that she'll tell the visitor about some local olive oil that is better than Loreto oil.

But before Anna gets to say more than a few words, the guest becomes very agitated. In English she asks Anna, "Do you think Georgio saw me?"

Anna points to the visitor's substantial, unique, brilliant yellow leather purse prominently displayed on the floor. "If he didn't see you, he saw your purse."

Too late, the visitor hides her bag between her chair and the garbage can. The conversation moves between English and Italian. For some reason, the more upsetting pieces are in English. So I learn that Georgio is the visitor's estranged husband, who left her after years of marriage. Feelings between them are bitter.

"It wasn't the best marriage, but it wasn't the worst, either. Why would he leave me? I heard that his father is ill. That must be why he's here. Should I visit his father?"

Wisely, Anna lets her guest talk. Any comfort the guest might have thought of providing Anna is long forgotten; it's now all about her tragic life and has nothing to do with Anna.

I smile to myself. Anna hasn't let on to me that she knows any English. The saga becomes background noise, and I fade out.

"Trust . . . in Him. He . . . is the light. He . . . is our saviour. *Sal-va-tion!*"

The choir is back. Today, the chorus is more animated, the rhythm syncopated. If I could move my feet, I'd be tapping them on the floor.

"A sinner came to me last night after our service. A sinner seeking the light. Seeking our saviour's guidance. Wanting to trust. Help him. Pray for him. He is sorely tempted by the sin of lust. The sin of the flesh. Pray for his wife. Pray for his children. And, yes, pray for the woman who beckons to him to sin. Let us all pray for them."

The choir quietly hums, responding to the cadence of the prayer. There is an exodus of footsteps, some of them passing by our door.

Anna gives a little curse. I turn my head to see her put her empty water bottle on the night table. There isn't a backup. Certain that the reason for her curse is that she is out of water, but that she has taken her abdominal support off for the night, making getting out of bed a tedious affair, I press my call button. An aide arrives and, holding a coin out to her, I ask her to buy a bottle of water. She points to the one on my night table. I gesture toward Anna. Willing, but a little perplexed, she takes the coin and returns with two bottles— giving one to me and one to Anna. Excellent. From the bed next to me comes a lovely "thank you"—the only two words of English she's spoken to me.

I'm exhausted, so exhausted that I have a ridiculous thought: "If I don't get some sleep, I'm going to get sick." How stupid is that? I press the call button and when the nurse comes, I ask for sleep medication.

7

SEPTEMBER 29

AT DAWN, the chickadee assures me that this morning breakfast will arrive. Sure enough, it does. A huge serving of yellowish semolina porridge, no sugar, no milk. Yuck. I don't try it. There's a small container of applesauce, which would probably taste good, but I discover I'm too weak to break the foil-top seal. A banana. Tea. The last two are my breakfast—if I can manage to get the skin off the banana, that is.

Things move a little slower on this ward than in the ICU. Or maybe it's just that there are only two of us in this room. I notice long pauses in activity. Not that I mind. The chickadee is quite entertaining. She seems to have a plethora of food nearby, returning to her perch to eat—allowing me to observe her patterns. First, she drops the food on the ledge. Then, she settles down, puffs her chest out, and pecks away at the food, eventually picking up a bit and finally swallowing by leaning her head backwards and then shaking her entire body from side to side. Then she looks at me, seeking admiration. Is this normal?

Ahhh. Two nurse aides arrive with a basin of warm water. It's been two days since my last bath and I stink. Truly stink. Rank with stale sweat from the agony of the drainage procedure yesterday. They investigate my cupboard, find the body wash, lotion, and hairbrush, and look for something else. They ask me, but I can't figure out what they want. Anna makes a suggestion. They smile, go into her cupboard, and pull out... towels, facecloth, toothbrush, and toothpaste. Uh-oh! I don't have those. They leave, taking the basin with them. Now what?

They return quite a while later, carrying the basin and some linen towels. I really hope they changed the water. A cold bath is not my idea of heaven right now. Chattering away, they pull the curtains around me, bring my bedside table within reaching distance, and plunk the basin down... and turn to leave. I get their attention to let them know that I cannot remove my nightie—too weak—and I can't bend—no stomach muscles— so basically all I can do is wash my face. They help, while making it very clear that it is time for me to be independent. Thankfully, they were thoughtful enough to bring warm water and a disposable toothbrush. I'm thrilled to brush my hair and teeth—myself. Independence is something I gladly seek.

They return to my cupboard, looking for something else, but the cupboard is empty. Holding their noses, they point to my nightie. With chagrin, I let them know I only have that one nightie. Just at that moment, Gordon walks in. Poor guy. Once again, he is confronted with the theatrics of Italian pantomiming. He gets the message—today's shopping experience will entail the purchase of another nightie and some towels. And he shows them as he makes a note in his Daytimer to bring my toothbrush and toothpaste tomorrow. Satisfied, the nurse aides leave. Anna chuckles, Gordon joins in, and I smile at them. Life in an Italian hospital when you can't speak Italian!

Gordon opens his iPad to read me all the messages he's received from family and friends back home. He has a tough time reading some of them, frequently choking up as the love and concern come pouring across continents and oceans to this room. I wish I could hold him, just for a moment, to let him feel my love for him, and I am so grateful to everyone for expressing concern for him as well as for me.

We talk for a bit, mainly about Marnie, who is in Europe and desperately trying to find a way to come to be with me. Gordon doesn't know that I'm actually glad that she can't get here—I'm just not strong enough to give her Philip's message, and I know that I must the moment I see her.

The procedure from yesterday has exhausted me. I drift off to sleep.

Gordon is gone when I wake. I'm so uncomfortable—in any position. It hurts to lie on my back because of the drain probes, but when I actually manage to roll to one side or the other, it hurts more. When I'm on the right side, where my ileostomy is, I feel like I'm compressing my entire intestines. When I'm on the left side, it feels like everything—I mean *everything*—is falling out. Either way it hurts.

But I'm getting the hang of my ultra-modern bed with its buttons—to change elevation and angle of head, back, sides, knees, and feet. The buttons work gradually so that I'm able to finally find a comfortable position. Slightly raised head, good lumbar support, raised knee support, and even a slightly elevated foot position. And my pillow has actually been placed in a comfortable position. I can hear Anna's gentle snore, so I know she is comfortable as well. Her deep breaths mark the passage of time.

A little man pokes his bald head through the door. He checks the door number and then looks at our beds. He comes farther into the room. In his arms is a basket of mauve orchids with deep pink throats—masses of blossoms. He asks a question I can't understand, but I'm sure he's asking for Anna, so I point to her.

"*No, no,*" Anna says.

"*No, no,*" the man says, then points at something that I can't see over my bed. With a grin and a wink he presents the orchids to me and then leaves. There I am in bed, swamped by orchids, absolutely sure that they must be for someone else. Who would send orchids to me in the middle of Italy? There must be a mistake.

Salvadore, my day nurse, comes rushing in. Apparently, he's heard about my orchids.

"*Magnifico. Molto magnifico!*" he exclaims.

His face is alight with pleasure for me. He finds a card nestled in the flowers and gives it to me. "With love from the Bowen Foundation Gang." I burst into tears. My friends from my home on tiny Bowen Island, nestled in the Salish Sea beside the city of Vancouver, British Columbia, have found a way to let me know they're thinking of me. A beautiful, beautiful way.

Salvadore puts his hands on my shoulders and leans close to me, his large, liquid caramel eyes holding my gaze, and in his deep voice repeats, "*Molto magnifico.*"

His broad mouth fully engaged in a generous smile, he gently takes the basket from my arms and places it beside my rose. The orchids have no scent, but Salvadore leaves behind a slightly spicy aroma—cinnamon and nutmeg, I think.

Within moments, there is a stream of visitors. All to see the orchids. Nurses. Doctors. Other patients. Visitors. "*Bello.*" "*Bellissimo.*" "*Squisito.*" Everyone has something to say about them. And my rose, too. And then there are comments about how lucky I am, how loved. They are right. I am.

In the midst of all this excitement, I don't notice that Anna is getting dressed. In street clothes. Her husband comes in, but before she leaves, she comes over to my bed and puts her hand on my shoulder. Her warm eyes and her soft voice wish me well.

She leaves. Our room, filled to overflowing only moments ago, feels much more than half empty now that Anna is gone.

Absolute silence.

Maybe I won't have a roommate for a while. Total privacy? That would be heaven.

Within seconds of that thought, a new roommate arrives, accompanied by two others. Her two daughters.

One daughter, tawny, like a lioness—an amber, sleeveless dress sheathing her generous curves, a golden belt dripping from her sumptuous but defined waist, golden thongs with glittering gems on the straps adorning her golden, orange-tipped toes. Golden hoops swinging from her ears. Jewelled black-rimmed sunglasses pushed back onto her head (dark roots showing through the tangled web of tawny, wild hair). A zebra-striped cellphone and a leopard-skin purse, both held by large golden hands with long iridescent orange fingernails, the fingers nearly invisible thanks to glitzy rings. Golden bangles on her arms that join her conversation as she roars into her phone. "*Ciao! Ciao! Ciao!*" Her arm moves as she speaks and the clatter of her bangles emphasizes her words.

The other daughter, dark and silent, like a black panther. She emits power—strong, silent power. But she is carefully nondescript. Dark hair. Just as tall, just as full, but not as flashy as her lionesque counterpart. Matronly almost in her simple, black-skirted, beige-bodiced linen dress and practical brown laced pumps. No bling for her. No nonsense.

And then the matriarch. From my horizontal vantage point, she is at least six feet tall. Maybe three hundred pounds. Immaculate. How can someone this enormous still move with such lithe grace? *She* does. She has a mannequin's face—perfectly defined by makeup that is perfectly applied on a face that is tight, unmarked by wrinkles, lines, pouches, or bags: large arched eyebrows; brilliant red lips, full and bowed; clearly delineated oval black eyes; and high cheekbones. Shiny dark hair sleekly surrounds her large vibrant face. Her silver-and-black jacquard robe slides around her as she moves with majestic ease. As she turns to sit on the bed, she removes her robe and I am astounded by her appearance from behind. An unkempt shapeless head of dull, grey-streaked brown hair. Her back and bottom, revealed by the open surgical gown, are misshapen by lumps and rolls layered one on top of the other. I am not trying to look at her; she is simply within my peripheral vision, which seems to be excessive these days. Can this possibly be the same woman?

Why is she here? Her surgical gown tells me that she must have already had some kind of procedure.

BBBLLLLUUGGGGGGGHHHHHEEEEOOOTTTGGG-HHH. The longest, loudest release of gas that I have ever heard emits from the matriarch. The term "fart" nowhere near describes what she has just released. (I have been to Africa, China, India, South America, Europe, and North America ... and I have been in recovery rooms after colonoscopies, but I have never heard anything like this.)

While the tawny one continues her phone call, a slender, youthful reproduction of the silent one enters, except she is not at all silent. Tall, dressed in fashionable, stretchy black, she is an epicentre of energy—all focussed on herself. The matriarch must be her grandmother, and I guess that the tawny one is her mother, based on the casual look they exchange.

When only the three women were in the room, they spoke a language I couldn't quite determine. But now they are speaking Italian. Well, the young one is. Rapid-fire Italian.

All about not being able to be here sooner, and a baby need-ing care, and why she has to leave in a moment.

BBBLLLLUUGGGGGGGHHHHHEEEEOOOTTTGGG-HHH.

BBBLLLLUUGGGGGGGHHHHHEEEEOOOTTTGGG-HHH.

"*Mio Dio!*" the young one exclaims.

She is shocked into an uncomfortable silence that is even-tually soothed by the dark one saying, "Poor Mamma. Can you imagine that she has been running her business all by herself all this time while she has been ill?"

Baby must be calling. The young one hastily says her goodbyes. Yes. Goodbyes. Not "*Ciao,*" not "*Arrivederchi.*"

The conversation among the three women reverts to their unfamiliar language.

Throughout all this, the privacy curtain between our two beds has been left open. I am exhausted by the unceasing en-ergy the women have brought with them and want the curtains closed. Seeking my call button, I find that the cord has come unhooked from my bed and I cannot reach it. The dark one sees my distress and comes to my bedside. She finds the cord and reties it to my bed, and then asks in English, "Help you?"

Grateful, I signal that I would like the privacy curtain drawn, which she does. She turns away, then turns back to me with a smile and asks, "USA?"

I respond, "Canada," and ask her, "Where from?"

She straightens, shoulders back, pride vibrating from her body. "Georgia—the *country*, not the state."

So now I know that I am hearing some kind of Kartvelian language. I know it isn't Russian.

I hear whispers, then some rustling, then three sets of footsteps leaving the room, the final sound another BBBLLLLUUGGGGGGGHHHHHEEEEOOOTTTGGGHHH.

"What can her problem be?" I wonder. It seems like an awful lot of gas if all she had done was a colonoscopy.

Lunchtime. I'm actually a little hungry—at least until I smell what it is: creamed tuna. Just the thought of fish makes me gag. The memory of Dr. Bing's question "Did you eat fish?" lingers (her unspoken thought—maybe a fish bone punctured your bowel—as clear as her question). Thankfully, there is also a heaping portion of pasta stars with olive oil on the plate. I eat every star, until the last one slips under the congealing tuna.

Gordon arrives and immediately unpacks his purchases—another pink nightie, just like the other one, *and* baby-blue pyjamas in the same lovely Italian knit cotton, with lots of tiny tucking around the neckline and the cuffs, *and* a butter-yellow bath towel, *and* two sunshine-yellow hand towels.

He is shunted out of the room. Marta, my favourite day nurse, and the young intern come in to examine my back, checking the bag for fluid drained from around my lungs. After the intern makes a quick phone call, she removes the bandage on my back, along with those irritating probes. Taking them out seems to be much simpler, and far less painful, than inserting them. They remove my catheter, too, and put on my clean nightie. Except for the medication and oxygen lines, I'm free. To do what?

Marta tells me that I need to start getting out of bed. Once again, I'm shown how to use the bed to assist me, but as soon as I put weight on my legs, I collapse into her arms. At that point, Gordon comes in and pantomimes that I need a walker to help support me. I'm left sitting in my chair, surprised at the swift turn of events.

Gordon replays an experience he had just outside the hospital. Apparently, he has been developing a non-verbal, very pleasant relationship with a panhandler who sits on the sidewalk outside the hospital. Every day, the fellow has a different array of essentials for sale, along with watches, bracelets, hairpieces. Every day, Gordon nods a greeting. The fellow nods back. Sometimes smiles are exchanged. Sometimes not. They have camaraderie, even though Gordon is not a customer. It's nice.

The events of the day are taking their toll. Sitting in the chair, which was such a treat not fifteen minutes ago, is now an effort. Although Gordon desperately wants me to try to walk, I know that today is not the day. He puts my yellow hand towel in the bathroom, then helps me back into bed, and almost immediately I'm asleep.

I wake to find dinner on my table. The sautéed zucchini is bland but palatable. I leave the white fish beside it untouched. Sleep beckons and wins over the usually irresistible hot tea.

I surface from time to time, hearing voices from my neighbour's area. Deep female voices. Cellphone rings and conversations. Nothing penetrates.

The sound of the choir enters our room.

"Trust . . . in Him. He . . . is the light. He . . . is our saviour. *Sal-va-tion!*"

The conversation next to me ceases.

And the now-familiar preacher's voice follows the sound of the choir. "Pray for him, for he has sinned. Can he not see what his children will see? Can he not see what his wife will become? Pray for him so that he might be saved. Pray for him."

The choir starts the slow chant: "Pray for him for he has sinned. Pray for him so that he will see. Pray for him to show him the way."

I feel like I'm listening to a soap opera on the radio. Except it is playing just outside my door.

"His children see their father with a woman, not their mother but a woman like they've never seen. They see him touch her like they've never seen their mother be touched."

"Hear their cries," sings the choir.

From one of the women next to me: "Ha! I wonder how the priest will twist this?"

So I'm definitely not dreaming this—my roomies hear it, too. What a relief!

An old woman comes in. I get just a glimpse of her in the doorway. She wears a long black skirt and a black shawl draped around her thin, bent body, covering her hair and much of her face. She is carrying something.

The greetings among the women are in a language similar to the one I've heard before, but this one is more guttural. Strangely, it seems more ancient.

There are sounds of bodies shifting, from chairs to the edge of the bed. Then a new sound. Similar to the sound my grandmother's hand-crank sewing machine made as she pushed the handle around, but this noise is accompanied by a whirring and clicking like the sound of several toy windmills.

Over this sound are the women's voices. They're still speaking their own language, but I can understand some of what they are saying. A message is spoken, and then the machine whirs. Another message is spoken; the machine whirs again. Messages of love. Messages of hope. Messages of next life. Messages of past lives. Messages from friends. Messages from strangers. Messages from family, from children, from enemies. It goes on for hours.

My imagination is taxed to the limit. What are they doing? If they were filling balloons, the room would be full. If they were making prayer flags, the line would reach out into the hallway and across the city. I may never know.

Finally, there is silence. Unbelievably, the silence is broken by the sorrowful sound of what I think is an alto saxophone. Since the entire ward is silent, the sound echoes everywhere.

I can hear the instrument being lowered into its case. Again, I hear the shifting of bodies. And then the old woman begins her story. I am swept away to another time, another place, along with the others in the room. Her voice is low, mesmerizing, like all good storytellers' voices.

"I was but a child when I heard about them. They were coming. No one liked us, but the people around us left us alone. We were useful to them. We could sharpen knives. We could tell the future. We could cure illnesses. But we were different, and they didn't like us.

"But the others that were coming. They *hated* us. Not just my family, but all our families. We had heard the stories. Stories about trains taking our people away. No one knew where they went, but we could *see death* for them.

"They were coming closer and closer. My mother knew. She could hear their bootsteps, the sound breaking her trance, silencing her sight.

"She must have given me a sleeping potion one night. When I woke, I was wrapped in an old carpet and it was covered in hay with vegetables on top. It was a farmer's cart. I could barely breathe, but something told me I shouldn't move, I shouldn't make a sound. I was there for hours.

"The farmer went to the market and sold his vegetables. He sold the hay, too. Then he slung the carpet over his shoulder and took it to someone else. I never saw that person. When it seemed safe, I climbed out of the carpet in the middle of the night. I was alone. There was some food and a sign that told me someone would come and get me. My cousin came. He was just two years older than me, but he knew a way over the mountains.

"So we escaped. But we never saw our families again. We saw the ones that hated us, though. And we caused them a lot of trouble. We were quick. We were quiet. We could empty the gasoline into our cans without anyone knowing, and then sell it. We could steal their food, and eat it."

Her voice is tired and trembling. "We left our childhood behind too early."

Whisper sounds. The footsteps of a tired old woman shuffling down the hallway. More shifting as three large bodies settle in on one hospital bed. More stories being told too quietly for me to hear. The murmur of their voices puts me to sleep.

I wake to an unfamiliar sensation. It takes a few moments to realize that I have a full bladder. Now what? Even if I had my support belt on, I know I couldn't make it to the bathroom.

Thankfully, the lovely night nurse comes quickly in answer to my call button. She is good at pantomime and immediately understands. Signalling me to wait just a moment, she leaves and returns with a bedpan.

There's a first time for everything, I guess. I've wondered how it is possible to lie flat on your back and pee without having it spread all over the place. Thankfully, that doesn't happen, but I'm surprised that even though I have a very full bladder not much is released. I call the nurse to let her know I've finished. With a smile and a quick shake of her head, she tells me to wait. Wise woman. Not long after, I'm able to pee a little more, and then a little later, some more. Strange. The nurse sees my puzzled look and explains with gestures that having a catheter in for a long time can make the bladder lazy.

Getting the bedpan positioned under me and then back out again has challenged both the nurse and me. Although it's the middle of the night, I can still hear the women next to me whispering.

The nurse does, too, and admonishes them, "*Silenzio!*"

The bed shifts under their collective weight and, surprisingly, they fall silent. I am soon lulled back to sleep by their soft snores.

8

SEPTEMBER 30

THE CHICKADEE and I wake at dawn. It's a special time for us. The little bird stretches and preens. I watch with envy, wondering if I'll ever have that flexibility and strength again. The bird looks at me, then nods. Is she saying, "Of course you will"?

A different kind of breakfast arrives: dry rusks, jam, butter, and hot tea. It takes a long time to eat. My jaw muscles have deteriorated, too, I guess. Certainly my coordination has—there are crumbs everywhere. These are noted by the two hilarious aides when they come to help with my bath and change my sheets. We all laugh when they mimic children with cookies in bed—and the strange places the crumbs can go.

They really want me to bathe myself, but when they see that I have trouble even getting the brush to the top of my head, let alone moving it through my hair, they relent, realizing that I am just too weak.

Gordon arrives, full of determination that I am going to get a walker today and start getting some exercise. He goes in search of someone to help him.

In the meantime, one of the day nurses comes bustling in. The fingertip oxygen monitor didn't get put back on after my bath; even worse, neither did the oxygen nose clip. She notices that my med bottles are empty. Out she goes and returns seconds later with four more—three she hooks up and the fourth is a replacement.

By the time Gordon comes back, I am clearly not going anywhere for an hour or more. That's how long it takes for the meds to drip through the line, and they are not on a portable trolley.

While waiting, I notice a new sensation—there's something kind of hot and heavy lying on my stomach. I manoeuvre my hand below the sheet and nightie and feel. Yes, there is something there.

"How stupid can I be?" I think. "It's the ileostomy bag. Of course, I'm eating now, so it's going to fill up."

Marta responds to my call. She closes the privacy curtains.

One look and she nods—it is time for it to be emptied. And while she's at it, she'll check the incision and change the dressing. She doesn't lower the head of my bed, so for the first time, I see it—all of it.

Reality hits me.

Hard.

The incision extends from my pubic bone through my belly button to my breastbone. The metal clips used to suture the incision are so regular and so precise they look like a steel industrial-grade zipper. Below my waist are other incisions, which have been sewn with transparent sutures. And hanging out on my right side is a semi-transparent bag, filled with the contents of my bowel.

As bodies go, I would never have won a beauty contest. But it is functional. My hips are wide, making childbirth easy. I've always had a flat tummy, thanks to all the sit-ups I've done.

My best attributes were my smile and great hair, but now my body has fully betrayed me. It is downright disgusting.

I am no longer the person I was. I never will be. Something extraordinary has happened to me—physically, mentally, spiritually.

Grief for my loss sets in.

Sensing my mood, Marta murmurs, comforting me, as she did when she held me while the drainage tubes were being inserted into my back. Her eyes are filled with compassion. If anything, her compassion makes my grief more intense.

But as she opens the privacy curtains, I dig down deep and hide my feelings from the man I love. The man who is so glad that I am alive. The man who is proudly displaying a "walker."

"Contraption" is my assessment of it. But it is a sparkling blue metal frame on wheels with crutch-like extensions on each side. It looks damned uncomfortable.

A physiotherapist saunters in and is astonished when I am still unable to get out of bed on my own. The med bottles are empty. So the first lesson is a thorough explanation of how to use all the buttons on the bed. It does everything but tip me out onto the floor.

After mastering that, the next step is to get some shoes on. Gordon retrieves some from my locker and puts them on me. My feet are so swollen, the buckles won't do up. Checking to make sure that they are not a safety hazard, the physio gives her assent.

I cannot stand up on my own, so she and Gordon help me rise, holding me upright until dizziness passes. They move the walker toward me so that I am in the middle of the U. She adjusts the arm supports to my height and tells me to take a step.

I have no idea how to do that. I look down at my feet,

willing them to move. Nothing. Meanwhile, the weight of my body resting on the arm supports is making them bite into my armpits.

I can't disappoint Gordon. I can't.

Hesitantly, reluctantly, oh so slowly, my left foot slides forward. Then my right foot slides forward. The walker moves, ever so slowly. One step. Two steps. I make it to the door. That's far enough.

But now a conundrum. How do I turn around? My brain simply cannot manage. Neither can my body. Gordon holds me upright and turns me, while the physio moves the walker into position. The few steps back to my bedside are exhausting, but, as tempting as the bed is, I ask to sit up in the chair for a while and am rewarded with the widest deep-to-his-heart smile I've seen on my wonderful husband's face for a very long while.

Dr. Lollio comes in. He explains that my white blood cell count is still high, so he's concerned about infection. He listens to my breathing and to my intestine, then checks the edema in my legs. He enters all his observations into his laptop, and then makes a call on his cellphone. Within minutes, someone arrives with a machine. Gordon is asked to leave while they do another ultrasound on my abdomen.

While all this is happening, Dr. Lollio shocks me by asking, "When would you like to leave the hospital?"

What an astonishing question. He's just told me that my white blood cell count is still high. I can't walk. I haven't used the toilet. I'm just barely starting to eat. I have no idea what I need to do with the bag attached to me. When would I like to leave the hospital?

"When will I be *able* to leave the hospital?" I reply.

"It is Sunday now, so maybe Tuesday, or Wednesday, or Thursday," he says.

"Good. Then let's make it Thursday," I say.

Dr. Lollio smiles, nods, and leaves the room.

When Gordon returns, he is as shocked as I am. We have been so focussed on each moment, we've given no thought to "after the hospital," though Gordon knows that the health insurance will expire five days after discharge.

I can't stay upright any longer. We manage to get me into bed—Gordon offering physical support while I operate the bed. Sleep comes immediately.

The clatter of dishes and a delicious aroma awaken me. Ohhh! That looks wonderful. A golden chicken thigh and leg. Pasta stars piled high with grated Parmesan. Grilled zucchini. The fragrance of rosemary and garlic and olive oil. The chicken falls from the bones in succulent pieces. The pasta holds the flavours of Tuscany. The zucchini adds a pleasant crunch. I eat it all. Every last pasta star. Every scrap of meat. Every morsel of zucchini.

I'm grinning like a well-fed cat when Gordon returns from his lunch break. He suggests that I have another walk. I reluctantly agree but am saved by the nurse arriving with an array of med bottles. Instead, we talk about going home. He's pretty excited. He went for lunch at the mall, where he found a travel agent.

Our excitement crashes. A cart is wheeled in. Another X-ray of my lungs. What is going on? An ultrasound this morning, an X-ray this afternoon.

Dr. Lollio comes back and tells us, "She has a sleepy stomach, but don't worry, that is normal."

Out he goes with no further comment. Gordon chases after him. He wants to know more and comes back to tell me that I still have fluid around my lungs but not enough to require the draining procedure again. He forgot to get an explanation of "sleepy stomach," but I don't really care. I know that some stuff is getting discharged into the ileostomy bag, so everything must be okay.

Now that the med bottles are empty, another walk cannot be avoided. I persuade Gordon that what would be absolutely wonderful for me would be to walk to the bathroom and to pee in the toilet. We get there, but I don't know how to sit down, so we have to call the nurse. How can sitting down on a toilet be so difficult? It should come naturally. But I don't have any coordination, or any muscle strength. So I have to be lifted down into the sitting position.

They leave me there, call button in hand. I wait. Nothing happens. I wait some more. Still nothing. "But my bladder is full. Why can't I let it go?" I wonder.

The nurse comes in. Understanding the problem, she turns on the tap, then leaves. Still nothing.

She comes back with a basin of water and puts my feet in it. I start to pee. She does a little dance in celebration. We both laugh and I pee some more. She leaves me.

Oh no. Now I have to get up off the toilet. There is no way. Fortunately, I don't have to use the call button. The nurse comes back and lifts me up. Using the walker, I shuffle over to the sink and wash my hands.

Then I notice my lovely new sunshine-yellow hand towel. It's lying in a soggy heap on the counter. I've never used it, but apparently it is now a communal towel for my roommate and her guests.

As I often do when drying my hands in a public washroom, I run my hands through my hair, using the moisture to crinkle my curls. This time, my fingers come out not only dry but covered with clumps of loose grey hair. I've heard that serious illness can cause hair loss. The discovery shatters me, plunging me back into grief. It is a long time before I can face leaving the bathroom.

Still standing in the walker and facing the sink, I can't figure out how to take a step backwards without falling over, but I need to make room to turn the walker around. I am confounded. Frustrated. Angry! How can I be this helpless? And I'm no longer close to the call button.

All I can do is whimper, "Gordon."

My voice, along with my strength, has all but disappeared. I have to stand and wait to be collected. Disturbed by the length of time I've been in here, Gordon arrives. By this time, I'm shaking with fatigue. Even with the walker, he has to provide extra support while I walk from the bathroom. There's no stopping at the chair. I need to lie down—and get this support belt off. My back hurts.

We agree to call it an early night. We're both exhausted from the day's ups and downs. Sleep comes easily, disturbed only by the arrival of a supper tray. The heaping mound of yellow mashed potatoes has no appeal. Sleep is much more attractive.

My troupe of roommates has returned, more animated than ever. The whirling sewing-machine sound buzzes at a faster rate, their voices keeping up with the sound. A phone clamours to be answered, and the matriarch's pronouncement, "He will come tonight. He promised," is greeted with excited laughter.

Where have they been all day? Who is coming?

I return to that inner space, leaving their voices behind.

The nurse comes, wanting me to use the toilet, but I'm too sore to move, so she grudgingly brings a bedpan. She busies herself with my nighttime meds, and then gets my pillow in a comfy position.

Lights out. I fall into a welcome, deep, dreamless sleep.

Sleep that is shattered by the sound of—yes—belly dancer finger cymbals beating out a sensuous rhythm, then suddenly clashing, not against one another but against something hard. I open my eyes. The light from the hallway silhouettes a pair of large bare feet in the air. They're connected to short, muscular, hairy legs attached to a naked male torso, flaccid penis flopping upside down against a hairy belly. I can't see his head. He is dancing on his hands. The noise I'm hearing must be from the finger cymbals hitting the floor. The women next to me are clapping to the rhythm and calling out to him—they sound like the catcalls one would hear in a strip joint. He disappears from view. Much ribald laughter. Then silence. Just in time. The nurse arrives with a scalding stream of angry Italian.

"Where is he?" I wonder. Did he hide under the bed?

The nurse leaves.

They aren't quiet for long. I hear purses being opened, then the crinkle of bills. The finger cymbals make a racket as they are stashed away. Someone leaves. I assume it's the dancer.

The women settle once more into that poor overburdened bed. My guess is that it's holding at least seven hundred pounds. Their voices return to last night's murmur—not a whisper, more a deep guttural monotone, in that same ancient language. It isn't the voice of the old lady tonight. It's the voice of the woman from Georgia—the black panther.

"It is happening again. The pogroms. This time it is the Chinese killing off our wanderers, chasing them from their ways on the paths they have always followed. It won't be long before they won't be able to cross the borders, and then where will they go? How will they live? Already, the rest of us are helping. We have two families living with us right now, but our neighbours are watching, and they don't like what they see. They don't trust us. The pogroms are coming to Georgia, too. I see it coming. I have the sight."

The voices become too low for me to hear the words, but the women talk for hours. I'm left to my own thoughts, and the dissent in Canada about the Roma—who aren't finding our country very welcoming, either.

Sleep is elusive tonight. When the nurse responds to my call in the middle of the night, I ask her to put a diaper on me so that she doesn't have to bring me a bedpan. She looks at me curiously and gestures, "Why?"

I don't want to be a bother for her.

"*Non irritante.*" She reassures me that I am not a bother, and that this is part of the care she must, and wants to, provide. She is so kind.

9

OCTOBER 1

———

I SEE THE first light of dawn this morning and my window companion fluffs her feathers.

Gordon arrives just as I'm finishing breakfast. He is wearing that determined look on his face. Whatever he has in store for me, I'm not going to be able to avoid it. He moves the upright torture chamber to the side of the bed.

"If you want to go home soon, you *have* to start getting mobile. Otherwise, you won't make it through the airports," he says.

Right at that moment, the nurse arrives with more med bottles. Seeing the look of thunder on Gordon's face, she scurries away, indicating that she'll be back "*mezz'ora*"—in half an hour.

Well, at least between us we're able to work the bed so that I'm neither exhausted nor in pain by the time I get onto my feet. Having to rest virtually my entire weight onto my armpits and the walker's uncomfortable supports, I manage to shuffle toward the door.

Going past my roommate and her daughters, I feel six pair of eyes watch my desperately weak journey. One of them murmurs, "*Corragioso! Excellente!*"

I reach the doorway and then continue out into the hall beyond! For the first time in nine days I have left my room on my feet. Before I can turn around and return to safety, Gordon sets a goal—"Let's just go to the nursing station. It's just another twenty feet."

I make it there. How am I ever going to get back?

The return trip is agony—my back hurts, my legs are like jelly, my armpits are on fire. But halfway back down the hall, my nurse passes by, nodding her approval of my efforts. That simple gesture buoys my spirits—and Gordon's, too. When we get back to the room, I ask to sit in the chair.

As he lowers me into it, he whispers, with a catch in his voice, "I'm so, so proud of you. Thank you!"

Gosh.

The meds arrive, and then soon after, someone new. This causes quite a commotion. Here I am, sitting in the chair, attached to all these bottles, and now I have to be moved back into bed for some reason.

Three nurses arrive. Two of them are my muscles, supporting me into standing position, guiding me to the bed, and lowering me to sitting position on the side of the bed. They shimmy me sideways into the middle of the bed, then lift my legs up and onto the bed. The third nurse manages the bottles and tubes, and then raises the head of the bed just in time to support my back. The curtains are whipped shut.

Escorted by Marta, the new person appears in my private space. He seems like a sweet young man. Round face. Gentle brown eyes behind black horn-rimmed glasses. Not tall. Not short. Not slim. Not fat. Nothing extraordinary. But likeable for some reason. Shyly, he tells me that he is the ostomy specialist, here to teach me how to look after my ileostomy.

Dear Lord, I'm actually going to have to touch it.

He asks Marta to raise my nightgown, remove the support belt, and arrange the sheet so that my private parts aren't exposed. After all I've been through, who cares? But then I guess it is as much for his modesty as mine, so I allow it to happen without comment.

And there it is. Bulging with liquid stool. So much for modesty. This may be his specialty, but it is my body. And right now I loathe it. He doesn't notice my reaction. He's busy inspecting it to see if it has healed properly and if the attachment is leaking.

Satisfied, he then looks at me. "The nurses have been emptying your ostomy all this time?"

I nod.

"I'll teach you how to empty it and clean it so that you can practise while you're still in the hospital. Then tomorrow, I'll come and teach you how to change the seal. I needed to see it so that I could bring the correct supplies. *Va bene?*"

I assume this is a rhetorical question, and I'm right.

Marta hands him a paper dish—a large version of a fish-and-chips tray. He puts it under the bag and shows me how to undo the latch on the plastic ring with one hand, while he holds the bag in position with his other hand.

I can barely sit up, let alone coordinate my hands. What on earth are they thinking?

The ring rotates under his guidance, and then the bag is free from my body. He raises the bag and puts it into the tray. Marta takes it and puts the whole thing into a bedpan, taking it away. What the hell am I supposed to do with the contents, especially since the hole in my gut is now squirting poop all over the bed linen, my only support belt, and my nightie, freshly laundered by Gordon just yesterday? This is worse than I could possibly have imagined.

But my sweet visitor is unperturbed. He tells me that I should never let the bag get that full, and that I will get to know when my gut is dormant, which is when I should empty it.

All I can think is that his comments are completely illogical—when my gut is dormant, the bag won't be full, so it won't need to be changed. Has *he* ever had a bag—oh, pardon me—ostomy?

He chuckles at the poopy mess everywhere and says that now I know I need to have toilet paper or a cloth nearby to cover the ostomy when the bag isn't in place. To emphasize his point, from his pocket he pulls clean, soft tissue paper and uses it as a cover. Well, that's a lesson I won't forget!

Marta brings him a dish of fresh, warm water and a clean, soft cloth.

"You must keep the area clean," he says, "but just with a damp cloth, nothing harsh. And don't rub. Be gentle. If you irritate the area, it will become very sore. But if you don't clean it, it will become sore, too. The stool is very harsh on the skin."

Then I remember how my mother used to clean hers. With soap and sometimes rubbing alcohol. She was so fastidious. Maybe too much so? She frequently found it painful.

He cleans the plastic ring on the piece of the apparatus that is stuck to my skin. The next step is to attach a new bag. There is a secret handshake, of course. And it requires pressing down on my stomach. This is nasty. The metal staples in the foot-long incision are uncomfortable as it is, but the additional pressure is excruciating, especially now that there is no muscle to resist, just flab like the Pillsbury Doughboy. He turns the ring, getting me to listen for the "click" that indicates a complete seal. Then he tells me to remove the bag and start all over.

My fingers are numb as they reach down to the bag. They fumble clumsily as I try to release the catch. First with my right hand. Then my left. I can't remember the technique. Gently, he holds my right hand and positions my forefinger on the catch, then presses it down. I can feel the release. He helps me turn the ring—counter-clockwise. The bag comes away. I grab some tissues and pat them onto the hole. He nods his approval, indicating that I should reattach the bag. I remove the tissues and hastily put the bag in place, but I don't watch for alignment of the catch. More poop squirts out onto the matching sealing rings. I have to clean everything—including the new bag—before I can attempt the attachment again. This time, I'm careful with the alignment, but I can't get the "click." Again, he guides my fingers into position, then presses my hand down while twisting clockwise. I hear the "click."

He smiles, nods, bows, and clicks his heels together in farewell. The nurses arrive to give me a second bath for the day and change the bed linens. Fortunately, Gordon had washed a second nightie, but now he has a foul laundry job to do tonight.

When the curtains are opened enough for Gordon to see, he can tell I'm exhausted. Trembling. Pale. Nearly incoherent. Now is not the time to suggest another walk. Marta indicates that he needs to buy another support belt before I can walk again anyhow. He decides to leave for a much-needed break. I need a nap.

I sleep through lunch, apparently. When I open my eyes, on my tray table is a congealing lump of something on a plate. It looks like more mashed yellow potatoes. I'm glad I didn't wake up for it.

Then I realize I woke because my roommates have returned. The matriarch, her two daughters, her granddaughter, and, yes, the old crone who was here the first night. It's the latter's voice that I hear.

"What the doctor has said is true. Last night, *I saw three black holes.* You need to prepare."

There is a long silence. And for the second time at the hospital, I feel palpable grief from a bedside next to me.

The silence is shattered by the matriarch issuing instructions. They are so rapid, I cannot make out the words, let alone the language, but it seems to be a combination of the ancient language, Italian, English, and yet another one.

There is a great bustling of bodies, purses, and coats, and the jangle of bracelets—then an exodus.

The matriarch sighs. Then she starts to talk into her phone.

"*Ciao… misurare… mortorio… vestiti. Per me… Grazie. Per mia figlia e mia nipotina… Quando? No, no—Oggi!*"

My seven years of Latin must be helping me understand what she is saying—or maybe it's the past ten days in an Italian hospital. She wants to be measured for her burial clothes, and her daughters and granddaughter to be measured for the clothes they will wear to the funeral. Today!

Gordon arrives at the same time as Claudia. Her generous nature showing, she delivers tea with one hand while clearing away my lunch tray with the other. It's not my usual afternoon tea but an early tea. Knowing that I haven't eaten anything since breakfast, Gordon patiently waits while I savour the golden liquid I've come to enjoy as much as the single malt Scotch that has been a tradition of ours on Friday evenings. The crisp, buttery biscuits add a simple—but now luxurious— bit of normality. As soon as I've finished, though, he puts my new support belt on. The med bottles aren't attached to me right now, so he's determined to get me out for another walk.

My underarms are raw from the walker arm supports, but I keep that to myself. Slowly, slowly, we make our way out of the room and to the nursing station. I decide that I want to see what is down the hallway on the other side, to the left. It is a long, wide, immaculate corridor, just like the one my room is on. This part of the hospital must be built in the shape of an H. The nursing station and some general rooms form the crosspiece.

Suddenly, I realize Gordon isn't with me. Scared, I manoeuvre a U-turn and head back. Gordon comes out of one of the general rooms. I see Dr. Lollio in there, sitting at his laptop.

We head back to my room. I'm not sure which hurts more, my legs or my arms. Most of me feels numb. But I have to pee. Well, here goes. Gordon is going to find out what it is like to get me on and off the toilet. We don't dance much—hopefully enough to make this work. I manage to keep the front of me covered with my nightie, so that he can't see the bag. I'm not ready for that. I ask him to leave and come back in five minutes. Stupid. Nothing—no pee. I need the water running. The call button is out of reach. I'll have to wait. No one can hear me. I hardly have a voice, let alone a yell. By the time he comes back, I'm so limp I'm almost falling off the toilet, but at least I peed.

We nearly have an argument. He expects to hold out his arm for support, and for me to use my arms to lever myself up. How can he not understand how weak I am? No arm strength. No leg strength. No stomach muscles. Overworked back muscles.

And then he confesses that he is afraid to touch me, to lift me. He doesn't want to hurt me.

We gulp back our tears of frustration and manage to get me upright and out of the bathroom. I decide to sit in the chair, instead of returning to bed. This surprises us both.

Gordon has an important question for me.

"When do you want to go home?"

"What do you mean?"

"Dr. Lollio still says that you can be discharged on Thursday, just like you wanted!"

"But that's only three days from now. Will I be ready?"

"He says that there shouldn't be any medical reason for you to stay longer. Basically, you are now healthy, just weak. He says you still have a bit of fluid around your lungs, but that will go away once you get more active. And he's sure the infection is gone."

"Then I want to be discharged on Thursday, if we can get flights home in time. Remember, our health insurance policy requires that we get home within five days of discharge."

"I remember. I think I mentioned that yesterday at lunch I found a travel agent. I could go and see what I can do. But I might not be back to see you today. Would that be all right?"

Actually making arrangements to go home? Not only would it be all right, it would be terrific!

Just as he is leaving, the troupe returns. They close the privacy curtain but not enough to block my view of the doorway.

No sooner do they get settled than a man comes in with a tape measure around his neck. He is very thin, with a narrow, hooked nose and an Adam's apple that appears to be helpful in keeping the tape measure in place.

The matriarch takes control of the conversation. The only words of hers that I can make out are *"nero," "non costoso,"* and *"grande."*

For each of these, his reply is: *"Naturalmente."*

But when the matriarch says, *"Grande,"* the granddaughter, who definitely likes her clothes skin-tight, exclaims, *"Non per me."* She is quickly hushed.

All of their measurements are being taken—the man muttering to himself as if he is calculating the amount of material required. It takes quite a while.

And then the matriarch asks the two questions I've been waiting for her to ask: "*Quando?*" (When?) and "*Quanto?*" (How much?).

The man seems unflappable as she responds to each of his answers with great hysterics. It is clear that I'm eavesdropping on two skilled negotiators. He has the upper hand on price. She has the upper hand on timing (after all, she is dying). I'm pretty sure that she agrees to a higher price than he originally quoted, but he has committed to delivering the clothes tomorrow morning. He won't leave until he's paid in full, though. I never knew what spittle sounds like as it spews out from an angry person, but now I do. The matriarch has just taught me. She demands once more that everything be ready by tomorrow morning.

He agrees and rushes out, cellphone in hand, already talking: "*Pronto. Si. Domani!*"

Marta comes in with more med bottles. She moves me into bed before she hooks me up, indicating that I should get some rest, closing the privacy curtain completely.

Rest. Nice idea, but my neighbours are talking non-stop. No murmurs today. Layers of voices. Conversations among the five of them. Phones ringing, telephone conversations woven into the ones in the room.

Now footsteps at the door: a new voice. A woman's. The focus turns to her, and once more, the matriarch takes charge. She is ordering food. I hear the number "*trecento*" (three hundred) and the words "*Mangiare. Molto.*" It sounds like food for a festival rather than a funeral. Maybe she is throwing a goodbye bash? I don't know anything about Roma customs. But it makes sense. If I had a choice, I'd rather be at my own wake, enjoying myself. What's the point in throwing a party after I'm gone?

The conversation goes on and on. "*Sì. Sì. Sì. No. No.*" Some good suggestions. Some not so good.

As entertaining as this is, I'm not getting any rest. The med bottles must be empty by now. I'll see if Marta can help me get onto my feet so that I can go for another walk. She isn't very pleased that I'm not going to rest, but she can tell I'm determined.

It's actually a relief to get out of there. I tell Marta to leave me once we get to the doorway. She asks me if I'm sure, and I tell her that I am. Earlier, Gordon had left me for a few minutes while I was walking and nothing happened. The only way I'm going to regain my strength and confidence is to walk. I need to retrain my muscles and my body. Balance and stamina. That's what I need. Oh, brother, just listen to me. I sound so strong, so tough. But my arms are shaking. Armpits rubbed raw by the walker. Feet ballooned beyond recognition.

Rather than walking the twenty feet to the nursing station, I head down the corridor just before it. It runs parallel to the one I took earlier. Behind double doors there is an immense room to the left. It looks like a waiting area in an airport— one designed for most people to stand. The walls are lined with a single string of bench seating. At one end is the vending machine where Gordon has gotten my water. And beside it is a telephone. That must be where those yearning calls were made from a few days ago. The room is so spotless and so empty I can understand why I could hear every word. Even my shuffling footsteps sound loud.

I do a full circuit of the room, and as I head back, I face two doors at the other end. The one on the right opens. I smell a non-hospital smell. Incense? Inside are a few people who appear to be in quiet prayer.

Curious, I edge forward to try to read the sign between the doors.

Fascinating. The first block of words is right justified—for the room on the right? The second block of words is left justified—for the room on the left?

Each block of information lists "*Servizi*" with different days and times. And each concludes with a different name and telephone number. Centred underneath the two blocks is the phrase "*Aperto 24 ore.*"

This must be where the church services are held. If the doors were left open during a service, I would be able to hear it while lying in my room. And the sign explains why I haven't heard a service for a couple of days—there wasn't one scheduled.

I've been upright for too long. Concerned, Marta comes searching for me and hovers while I inch my way back to my room. But on my way, I notice for the first time that there is a room between mine and the big waiting area. Peeking inside, I see that it is a small meeting room. No wonder I could hear the exchange between the priest and would-be sinner. I'll bet they met here—for privacy—rather than in the big meeting area. Little did they know!

The pieces of my physical environment are forming into a whole. All that remains is the source of the food. I smell it cooking sometimes, so I'm pretty sure there is a food prep area on the floor.

Just as I reach my room, the door directly across the corridor bursts open. My four Roma friends tumble out—being escorted by one short but extremely strong, square, and assertive Claudia. She's making something very clear. From Claudia's hand motions, I gather my roommates—all of them—wanted to be served supper in our room. And I gather that Claudia is not prepared to be a waitress, or to clear up after them. *No, no,* if they want to eat together, they eat over there, and her gesture tells them the way! (I smile to myself, remembering Anna and her husband enjoying their meal together. Sofia brought her father's tray of food. She must have taken the tray away, too.)

Marta and I manage to make it through the doorway ahead of the gang. They are furious! Each of the voices layered one on the other fills the range of a staccato aria. Mezzo-soprano, alto, tenor, even bass! Up and down the scales of outrage. What a performance. And then the phones start to ring, clattering on the hard surfaces, rattling inside purses. "*Pronto.*" "*Pronto.*" "*Ciao.*" More voices come into the room from the cellphones as everyone tries to make themselves heard. Marta wants to instill some quiet, but I indicate her efforts would be futile right now. She understands, nods, and then leaves.

As the daughters move between the two beds, their large bodies shift the privacy curtain from side to side, opening it inch by inch. Eventually, I have full view of the doorway, and partial view of all the antics. Some of the clattering that I have been hearing has been bracelets chattering against one another as arms wave in the air, emphasizing each point. On the lioness, gold bracelets with charms—reminiscent of the dull rattle from the casting of bones I heard when I was in Africa. On the black panther from Georgia, silver bracelets with coins—shimmering tinkles ending in emphatic clacks.

Their backs are to the doorway, so I see him first. A tall black shadow of a man, made taller by his black hat and long black jacket. His beard is long, bushy, black. As he enters, I see his perfectly curled *peyos*. (Long sideburns, curled. Typical of Orthodox Jews.) What is *he* doing *here*?

Oh, to be a linguist! The women are speaking that ancient guttural language. There is a sense of urgency in their voices.

He interrupts. "I am not a rabbi."

Does he understand their language? Could it be a derivative of Yiddish?

What *is* he doing here?

"*Quando?*" he asks.

"*Non lo so,*" the matriarch replies. Then, very quietly, she says, "*Presto.*"

The bold one, the lioness, asks "*Quanto?*"

Once again, there is a feverish negotiation, but I have no idea what price they settle on. I know they come to an agreement and only partial payment is required right now. After some rustling of bills, he steps back into my view. Still facing into the room, he stiffly bows toward them, and then leaves.

When I get out of hospital, I need to learn about Roma culture. What on earth has just transpired? It sounds like they have asked someone from outside their own culture to conduct the matriarch's funeral rites. I'm a preacher's kid. Many hours of my youth were spent with my ear to the heat register, listening to my father's conversations with his parishioners. He didn't charge for his work, but I know what funeral planning sounds like.

Claudia arrives with a dinner tray for me—eggplant parmigiana. I hope it is as good as the one I make at home—a favourite of mine. While she settles it on my bed table, the women exit and walk toward their dinner. Hearing them, Claudia looks at me and grins. She won!

Although Gordon would want me to go for an after-dinner walk, the quiet of the room enfolds me. I savour the rare moment alone.

The chickadee has brought a piece of straw and is trying to peck at it as if to make it stick to the window ledge. Does she want to make a nest? The straw falls away, but my little companion is undaunted. The bird retrieves the straw and eventually impales it in the window seal. I marvel at the ingenuity of earth's small creatures, and the precarious places they call home. Hardly a parallel, but right now, this bed, this part of the room, is my home.

My peace is broken by the return of my roommates and their steady stream of intense chatter. The contrast is too much, motivating me to get up and walk. At that moment, a new night nurse appears, asking if I need anything. She helps with the stiff lever on the chair, lowering the footrest so that I can awkwardly manoeuvre myself into a standing position. I forget to remain still for a moment. Dizziness strikes. As I stumble, she catches me before I collapse. Once more, I am held in strong arms, comforting arms. I am overwhelmed by the kindness I have experienced here, in this hospital, in Italy. We are so fearful of touching in Canada we've forgotten the healing that touch provides—a profound loss.

Curiosity takes me back toward the rooms I think are chapels. I can't remember which one should have a service right now, but I think one does. But it is too far. My legs are too wobbly, and even worse, my armpits are raw. I have to return to my bed. The nurse sees me and hurries to help. I guess I look, again, like I'm going to collapse, with an added tightness of pain on my face that I cannot conceal.

My bed is welcoming, especially once the support belt is removed—the nurse has strong arms but is so very gentle. Sleep comes quickly.

I'm not sure what wakes me. The hallway is dark. The streetlight that I often see reflected in the window is off, so it must be the deep quiet of late at night, when no motion activates the streetlights. Of course, I need to pee. Luckily, the call button is firmly attached to the side rail. With the new nurse, I have to pantomime what I need. She offers to get me to the bathroom, but I pantomime what would be involved.

She understands, brings the bedpan, and then comes back to retrieve it without my asking.

I close my eyes, expecting to fall right back to sleep. Instead, I hear the low murmur of voices from the next bed. The voices are muffled, but I detect the tones of the old woman from the first night. There is a pattern, a rhythm, to what she is saying. And there is repetition. An incantation. After a while, I can make out distinct syllables, which soon become words—some of the words I understand, though I don't believe what I'm hearing.

I'm pretty sure she is casting a spell—an exorcism of the evil that has invaded the matriarch's body.

The granddaughter asks a question. The answer confirms what I have guessed, and it shocks me.

"*No. No.* Like this. Wrap the thread around the maggot's head until his eyes pop open. Like this . . . *Sì. Sì.* Like that."

The granddaughter asks another question.

There is a cackle—yes, a cackle—a rough chortle. Then the answer: "Cow dung and feather beds."

The chanting murmurs hypnotically on and on. With each repetition, I get edgier. Worried. The occult always makes me nervous. Deep down, I believe in its power. My first experiences were as a teacher in Africa, with the young students telling me about visits with their families overnight. This was physically impossible, as their families were hundreds of miles away, unreachable by telephone, and this was long before virtual visiting via the Internet. On more than one occasion, though, the school received telegrams or letters with descriptions of the family death or illness or birth that were identical to the information already relayed by the student. African science, the students called it.

If the women are performing an exorcism, where is the evil supposed to go? Is it being destroyed or just exorcised from *her* body? Do my roommates care? Is the evil drifting into me?

If there was ever a good time for a prayer of protection, this is it. Do I have the ability to meditate, to visualize an aura to protect me, or to pray for help? All I can manage is a simple heartfelt request: "Please protect me with Your love."

Exhausted, I fall asleep.

10

OCTOBER 2

W HEN I WAKE, they are gone! The matriarch and her daughters must have packed up and left while I slept.

Standing at the now-vacant bedside, Claudia is furious. Glaring at me, she spits out the word *"vermi,"* slamming her hands on the mattress encrusted in soiled sheets. I know she's seen the maggots. Two orderlies come into the room. The entire mattress, with all of its linen, is put into an enormous plastic bag, tightly sealed, and removed from the room. Is it going to an incinerator or sterilizer?

I'm relieved that I wasn't imagining the whole scene last night. But how bizarre!

And if the mattress has to be destroyed, what a waste. Hospital mattresses are incredibly expensive, especially the ones I've had—state-of-the-art massaging mattresses that circulate air around the patient to eliminate the risk of bedsores and are adjustable for patient comfort. But from the cleanliness I've seen here, I know that no maggots are welcome in this hospital—certainly not under Claudia's watch!

Gordon arrives. I am so happy to see him. He brings the walker over with a determined look in his eyes. A look that is matched in my eyes.

"No more walker for me," I declare. "My armpits can't take it. I'm going to have to manage on my own."

His expression is priceless—completely stunned!

Slowly, slowly, I shuffle out of the room with Gordon right beside me, ready to offer support if needed. Now fully bearing my own weight, I am conscious of the force of gravity on my insides. Without stomach muscles to counteract gravity, I feel like everything is going to drop out of me. Now I understand why women who have had Caesarean sections hold on to their stomachs as they walk. But if I do that, I'll fall over. Having been horizontal for so many days, my balance is terrible. I need my arms. We make it to the nursing station but no farther. The walker may have been uncomfortable, but it did offer support.

Back in my room, we have precious privacy. Gordon tells me that the travel agent was able to book us on Lufthansa, business class, leaving Florence on Monday and leaving Frankfurt on Tuesday.

We're going home!

"Thank you for the business class. I didn't want to ask, but I really don't think I could manage being squished into an economy seat."

"There was never any question in my mind. No matter what it cost, you were going home business class—at least."

"Did it cost a small fortune?"

"No. But it did take a lot of persistence—by me, and by the travel agent. Getting one-way fares was going to be outrageously expensive, but we got return tickets at less than half the cost of one-way tickets!"

After Gordon left the travel agent, he went back to Santa Maria and talked to Laura and Stefania about our plans.

When they found out how weak I still am, they suggested that we move to a different apartment—a ground-floor, two-bedroom apartment. So that's what he did—packed us up and moved us in. I hadn't even thought about those twenty steps. Once again, I'm overwhelmed by Italian kindness.

I ask Gordon to tell me about Stefania. I had only met Laura.

"As you know, they are sisters," he says, "and they share the management of Santa Maria. Laura isn't usually there as much as she has been recently, because she has another job as an event coordinator at a resort nearby, but Stefania has a new baby and is working less. Their father, Giuseppe, is also involved. He does the maintenance, but his pride and joy is the garden."

We decide to go for another little walk. This time, I proudly shuffle to the chapels, showing Gordon where they are. He hadn't noticed them when he got my bottled water from the vending machines. I'm starting to feel like the hospital is my home. When we get back to my room, Gordon leaves but promises to return after lunch.

He misses the excitement. At the same time as my lunch, some kind of inedible-looking cream soup, another roommate arrives, bringing yet more drama. She is elderly, weeping, screaming with anger and frustration, waving her arms frantically in the air, stubbornly resisting even entering the room, let alone lying down. With her is a man perhaps in his forties, and he is very calm, very firm, quite skillful at avoiding confrontation, though I can see it is difficult for him. Not a doctor—perhaps a son?

A woman about the same age as the man walks in. The elderly woman, previously frantic, now becomes hysterical. Within moments, the newcomer cowers and retreats backwards out of the room so that the elderly woman is just barely out of reach; otherwise, she would have struck blows, and those blows would have hurt.

"Mamma, Mamma," the man soothes. "Shh, shh."

Sobbing, Mamma lowers her voice but babbles on—still in hysterics—in a mix of Italian and English. "She has no right to bring me here. I am fine. All I did was fall. I don't need help. I don't want help. *Get me out of here!*"

A doctor arrives and approaches but doesn't get very near. Those hands are weapons, and the doctor is obviously experienced enough to know to stay away. He retreats from the room.

Gradually, the son is able to soothe his mother, talking slowly and calmly. He wants a doctor to look at the bruise on her temple and on her back, where she fell. He asks if they hurt. Frightened, the woman admits that they do—as does one on her shoulder and one on her hip.

She finally agrees to let a female doctor—a *dotoressa*—examine her.

Clearly, the son has been in a hospital before. Without hesitation, he reaches over and presses the call button. Within moments, a nurse appears. Confidently, the son explains the situation.

"*Certo*," the nurse replies and hurries away.

When she returns, she brings with her the same doctor who arranged for Gordon to have his blood pressure medication prescription refilled. She is just the right person for this situation. Tiny. Calm. Strong. Practical. Graceful. Classically beautiful. A person in charge. A *dotoressa*. Mamma quickly succumbs to her competence.

I would have left earlier, but there was too much confusion around the doorway for me to exit safely. I do now. I shuffle to the big waiting area and even manage to lower myself onto one of the cold, hard, orange plastic bench seats. The cavernous room is empty, except for me and the hum of the vending machines. It's been a long while since I've had so much space to myself. I feel small, cold, even a little naked.

A "chapel" door opens behind me. The scent of incense mixed with candle wax wafts out, a warming, comforting smell. The door shuts with a quiet whoosh and silence, with the vending machine hum, is my companion again.

Knowing it is too soon to return to my room, I decide to explore farther down the hallway. New territory for me to conquer! It is another arm of the H configuration—an extension of the hallway where my room is. I pass an equipment room where wheelchairs and walkers are stored, a room where cleaning carts are stored, a room filled with clean linens, and then a series of patient rooms just like mine. All spotless and completely uncluttered.

I hear a noise behind me. Carefully, I turn to look and see a woman standing on what looks like a miniature Zamboni. She is washing the floor. She indicates that she'll be coming back up on the side where I am walking. I need to get out of the way. She has a job to do. What an efficient way to keep the corridor spotless, but it is only possible because there is no clutter.

Making it back to the crosspiece of the H just in time, I go to the nursing station to ask if things have calmed down in my room. I had felt like an intruder earlier. The nurse is more worried that I won't be able to get back under my own steam. I confess to feeling kind of wobbly, so I'm glad for her firm arm around my waist, piloting me back to my bed. It's definitely time for a nap.

When I open my eyes, Gordon is sitting in the chair, playing a game on his iPad. Just as he shifts his chair over into visiting position, the ostomy specialist arrives. It's time for more training. And he indicates that Gordon should be a part of it.

Oh, brother! Just what I need is to have my husband looking at this grotesque appendage on my deformed belly. Really.

"Is this necessary?" I ask.

The specialist is quite firm. He wants to make sure that if I forget something, I have someone else to ask.

So the privacy curtains get whisked around, and there we are, the three of us, looking down at my mutilated body. The training begins.

From his doctor's satchel, the specialist pulls out a ring. It is beeswax, sandwiched between two pieces of waxed paper. It looks like a miniature seal used between a toilet and the floor. That's what this ring is for, too, to make a "leak-proof" seal to attach the bag to my body.

But wait. One size does not fit all. I have to measure my ostomy opening and then cut the hole in the ring to fit. It can't be too small because the beeswax will irritate the mucous tissue that is part of the ostomy opening. But it can't be too large because the gunk that my intestines emit is quite corrosive, so I wouldn't want it to come in contact with my skin. Oh! And just in case I think I could cleverly cut many rings and have a ready supply on hand, I can't do that because the opening will shrink over time. So the best thing to do is cut the hole when I need a new ring.

Okay. So how do I measure it? He has a set of patterns that I try on for size. But that means taking off the bag—and taking off the existing ring. Great. So this will get messy, right?

Yes, indeed, it will. The existing ring has to be peeled off and it leaves a sticky, gooey, liquefied beeswax mess (an indication that it was time it was changed). Warm water gently sponged over the area cleans it off pretty easily, though.

At least this time the specialist is armed with a lot of tissues to cover the ever-emitting hole. Doesn't cover the smell, though. Poor Gordon. He hasn't even changed a baby's diaper, and now he has to breathe in this noxious odour. I look up at him and am amazed to see him taking pictures—recording everything the specialist is teaching us. That helps me relax. He's here, with me.

Then the specialist points out that it isn't as simple as making a perfect circle. Nope. My ostomy is more like an oval and I need to adjust his patterns accordingly. He hands me the new ring, the proper pattern and a pen. I'm supposed to trace the circle from the pattern and then make adjustments to it to my oval shape. Then he hands me scissors, indicating that now it is time to cut the shape. He must be joking! My fingers have no strength and my hands shake. Eventually, he realizes that it truly is an impossible task, so he relents and does the cutting.

Now for attaching the ring to the skin. There are two sides to the ring. One side is specifically designed for the skin, the other specifically designed to stick to the latching mechanism that holds the bag in place. He's pretty clear that I shouldn't get them mixed up; otherwise, the "leak-proof" seal won't be so leak-proof. We pay special attention to this part, and I hear the camera shutter clicking.

Who invented these gizmos? As the specialist shows us how to peel off the paper, the ring immediately becomes more elastic—and sticky. Even he has to work to get it placed into exact position without a finger underneath. I find putting Band-Aids onto myself nigh on impossible without getting one part stuck to the other rather than onto my skin. How on earth am I going to manage this seal of Silly Putty?

Now comes the latching mechanism. Can I just put it on randomly? Oh no. It needs to be positioned "just so," so that when the bag gets attached it falls diagonally across my abdomen and not vertically down onto my leg. And once in place, *press down.* Oh. My. God. Did he forget that I have just had abdominal surgery? Pain, quite dormant until now, shoots through me.

Unperturbed, the specialist carries on with his explanations, and then hands me the bag to attach. Although I follow his instructions, it does not click in place. A gush of disgusting body emissions leaks out through the seal. Cleanup is required. When I attempt to latch on the bag a second time, he puts his hand on top of mine and says, "Counter-clockwise." That was my problem. It is counter-clockwise from his vantage point but clockwise from mine. While it turns, he pushes down, something I am loath to do. But there is a satisfying "click," so I know I'm safe from mess for a while.

As he is putting away his tools, he asks if we have any questions. I do.

"Will I have enough supplies after discharge from the hospital to get me home?"

He asks, "How many days?"

"Six," we respond, knowing that it will take a few days even after we're home to find what we need.

He shrugs but indicates that he will do whatever he can.

"And do you have an extra pair of scissors that I could have? Yours seem to be designed specially for ostomies."

Again he shrugs, but I have a sense he'll find something for us to use. He leaves as quietly as he arrived.

Mamma next door is snoring loudly. Gordon and I decide to walk for a bit.

This is my third walk of the day. Bravely, I agree to try to push myself. Gordon is clearly concerned that I won't have enough stamina for the trip home. I think he is also worried that he is going to be my sole caregiver very soon, and that neither of us is ready. He's probably right.

We manage to cross in front of the nursing station and head down one of the long hallways, but halfway down I have to turn around. My legs are shaking and I lose my balance. Gordon tries to support me by taking my arm, but that isn't enough. He has to put his arm around my back, lending me his strength and balance, half-carrying me back to the room. We are both glad to get me there. He is scared. I hurt.

Once I'm settled in my chair, Gordon goes to his knapsack on the floor and pulls out my iPad and earbuds.

"I thought you might be ready to listen to some Bocelli tonight. You downloaded all of his music to listen to in Italy and you haven't had a chance to listen to even one song."

His thoughtfulness is overwhelming. All I can do is nod my thanks.

Shortly after he leaves, music comes down the corridor. Tentative single notes from an organ, accompanied by the humming of a pleasant baritone voice. Words are added as the notes are played more confidently.

"Rejoice in Him. Believe in Him. Hallelujah! Hallelujah! He is the one!"

And then the music stops.

Or maybe I just can't hear it over the commotion next to me. My new roommate is thrashing about in her bed. Her heart monitor is beeping frantically. Just as I'm about to press my call button to get help for her, there are footsteps at the doorway. I hear a nurse's voice and soon there are others. No one seems to be frantic, but there is a lot of action. I have no idea what is happening.

Seeking privacy for my roommate and for myself, I manage to manoeuvre the iPad closer to me and plug in the earbuds. But for some reason I can't get the audio turned off so that the music only comes through the earbuds. This is *so* frustrating! Exhausted, I give up.

The son's voice enters the room, along with an unfamiliar woman's voice. They are having a conversation about my new roommate as if she weren't there. But she makes her presence known.

"*Silenzio! Lo non sono stupido!*"

In response, the son makes soothing sounds, but my feisty roommate will have none of that. Hastily, both her visitors leave. Unbelievably, I hear her give a snort, then a chuckle. Is this health crisis of hers a ruse to get attention from her family?

Supper is simple. Pasta stars with wonderful olive oil and Parmesan. It is addictive.

The aides come to help me get ready for the night. Taking off the support belt is a welcome relief. Although it is essential for standing and walking, it is so constricting that sometimes it is hard to breathe, especially when I'm sitting or lying down.

I'm not ready to sleep, though, so I focus on the dots on the floor, imagining what shapes are there, like one does sometimes when looking at the clouds. The dots are so random and interesting that I had Gordon take a photo of them, thinking that if I had to be here for much longer, perhaps Ella and I could use the dots to play a FaceTime game of I Spy. Wouldn't that be something—me in a hospital in Italy and four-year-old Ella in Red Deer, Alberta, playing a game together?

The music begins again. The organ and the baritone voice. He sings the refrain once, and then a choir repeats: "Rejoice in Him. Believe in Him. Hallelujah! Hallelujah! He is the one!"

At first they sing quietly, as he did, but gradually, the tempo quickens and the sounds crescendo. A rhythm is added. All the voices are female in delicious harmony. It is a joyous, celebratory song. Then silence. I want more. I want to go to where the music came from and find out when I can hear more. But I'm in bed, and without the support belt, I can go nowhere.

Sleep doesn't come this night. When my eyes close, the dots from the floor flit across my eyelids—teasing, dancing, merging into fleeting shapes, leading me to memories created in good health.

Dots becoming two sets of feet climbing Mount Kilimanjaro, mine clad in rubber boots, the porter Emmanuel's strapped with strips of rubber tire. Dots becoming white paper crowns worn by the Young Swimmers singers at Msalato Girls School—slide-stepping and swinging to African songs, their hands and feet providing syncopated sound as their beautiful voices melt in harmony. Dots becoming marigold petals scattered at the feet of a bride and groom at their wedding in Mumbai. Dots becoming candlelit magnolia-leaf boats floating at dawn on the Ganges at Varanasi—one of them sent on its way by me with a prayer for my mother, who had recently died. Dots becoming canoe paddles dipping into the rivers of Canada that Gordon and I have canoed—small and large, from the St. Croix in New Brunswick to the Nahanni in the Northwest Territories. Dots becoming babies—the beginnings of the family I love so.

The memories are rich. My life has been full. Although sleep is elusive, the night passes easily enough.

11

OCTOBER 3

———

A T DAWN, my little window-ledge friend pecks at the window and then flies off. She returns when morning light is filling the sky. She has something in her mouth, which she drops onto the ledge and pecks away at. Breakfast. Finished, she fluffs out her chest feathers and settles, head tucked in. It is October—the mornings must have a chill in the air. Following her example, I nap until my breakfast tray arrives.

As I am eating my dry toast and jam, sipping fragrant golden tea along with it, Claudia comes in carrying a clipboard. She thrusts the clipboard in front of me and asks me a question. I have no idea what she is saying, but I look at the paper on the clipboard and recognize it as a hospital menu. She must be asking what I want to eat today. Wow! I must be getting better. Thankfully, my glasses are nearby. Even with them on, focussing on the tiny print is difficult.

Looking down the menu, I'm delighted to see all of my hospital favourites: roasted chicken, zucchini, pasta with oil and Parmesan, pasta with tomato sauce. Zucchini is available for both lunch and dinner, so I check it twice. When Claudia notices, questioning my double selection, I rub my tummy and lick my lips to suggest that I think it is delicious. She laughs. She should do that more often. It is a boisterous laugh that makes me laugh, too. It doesn't matter that laughing hurts; it is lovely to share that moment with her.

She looks at my breakfast tray and notices that I haven't eaten my fruit—that revolting canned fruit salad with soggy grapes that every hospital seems to serve. I stick my finger into my mouth and make a vomiting sound. She finds this hysterical. She picks up the cup of fruit and walks out, barely able to make it to the door in a straight line because she is laughing so hard.

Moments later, she is back with some applesauce. When I pick it up, she motions that it is hers, it came from her own "*pranzo.*" Claudia has a warm heart beneath that brusque, tough persona.

"*Grazie, grazie*" is all I can say.

It is enough. She nods her head, smiles, and leaves me to enjoy my applesauce.

Gordon arrives. He looks different today. His posture has changed. He has an air of purposefulness. No wonder.

He says, "I need to get you out for a good walk, and then I have to spend time with the administration department to get all your discharge papers in order so that they will be acceptable for our health insurance coverage. No time to waste!"

My support belt isn't on yet, so we decide that now is a good time to figure out how to put it on ourselves. Oh, boy! Our first attempt is a disaster. We don't coordinate our movements. When there needs to be a gap between the mattress and me so that Gordon can slide the belt under, there is only the firm line of my body. And when we finally get the belt slipped under and around me, it is upside down, so the Velcro fasteners cannot connect to secure the belt in place. Getting it back out is equally difficult. Sweating, we decide to take a few moments before trying again. We don't say a word to one another during that break, but I know he's thinking the same thing I am—"Please don't let this be an omen for when I'm discharged."

Our next attempt is an amazing series of smooth motions. In less than a minute the belt is on, fastened, and perfectly positioned. Now that's the omen I will hold on to.

We manage to use all the capability of the bed to help ease me out, and I remember to move slowly from sitting to standing to taking the first few steps. Recalling my walk with him yesterday, Gordon puts his arm around me. Surprisingly, I don't need his support for balance. We walk slowly, steadily, in front of the nursing station and then left, down the long corridor that we had tried to explore earlier. All the way to the end, and back. And then around the corner to the chapel area.

Just as I am about to tell Gordon about the music I heard last night, Dr. Lollio comes rushing out of the doctors' room. I'm left to walk back to my room by myself as Gordon and Dr. Lollio walk away, discussing something about my discharge.

My room is filled with people. Mamma's son, a woman (perhaps the daughter-in-law), *Dotoressa*, a nurse I don't recognize, and another doctor are all talking at once. The only silent one is Mamma. I'm pretty sure there's going to be an outburst from her—she does not like to be ignored. Sure enough, she starts to wave her fists in the air and shouts. I have no idea what she is saying, but the rest do. I close the privacy curtains before sitting in my chair, but that doesn't block out the sound. Sounds of anger, fear, frustration, calm, pleading. So many emotions. The calm voice wins out. I think it is *Dotoressa*, speaking directly to Mamma.

Eventually, Mamma says, "*Sì.*"

I can actually feel the shoulders in the room relaxing.

Now the conversation moves from one of convincing Mamma to one of organizing and instructing Mamma, Son, and everyone else as to exactly what is going to happen. A telephone call is made, ending with, "*Ora!*" Within moments, I hear the rattle of a technician arriving with a cart to take blood samples. And Mamma is completely docile through it all—for now.

Gordon comes in and explains that he's now going to the administration office to start the paperwork for my discharge tomorrow.

Conversation starts up again next to me. Son is persuading Mamma to let Sister come in and see her. Mamma starts to get distraught, but Son soothes her. In English, he explains that both he and *Dotoressa* believe that Sister called the ambulance because it was really needed. And then he switches to Italian, but the meaning is clear: Mamma, you are ill; we are worried. ("Mamma . . . *malato* . . . *preoccupato*.")

All of her bluster leaves her with his next sentence: "*Mamma, noi ti amiamo.*" We love you.

She agrees to allow Sister to come in. The privacy curtains are open just enough for me to glimpse Son bringing in Sister—the same woman who retreated, whimpering, the first day Mamma was here. His arm is around her shoulders, protecting her. Her face is wet with tears. She tries to speak but can't. There is a long moment of silence, then a shuffle, then murmuring. I hope they are in each other's arms, reconciling.

Claudia brings a lovely cup of tea and some biscuits. How did she know? A night of no sleep, a long walk, and the emotion of the family next door have left me drained. Thirsty, too. She rubs her tummy and licks her lips, then grins. She hasn't forgotten our exchange yesterday. And she must have observed my pleasure in a cup of tea. My smile of thanks lights up her face.

When Gordon comes in, my eyes are shut, but I know the sound of his footsteps, and these ones are happy footsteps, not worried ones. Sure enough, when I look at him, his face is relaxed and full of anticipation. His meeting at the administration office went well. They are preparing the discharge papers exactly as required by the insurance company and consulting with him to make sure that they are doing all that is necessary. What a relief. Our experience with insurance companies has been less than stellar. As a rule, they are not flexible in interpreting their policies, so our claim has to be perfect.

Realizing that I leave tomorrow, we talk about what purchases are needed for the transition. I disguise my trepidation by focussing on the shopping list. Top of the list is adult diapers. This a surprise for him.

"You're not wearing them now, are you?" he asks.

"No, the nurse brings a bedpan two or three times in the night. Without the support belt on, I can't get up, and I'm worried that you will get exhausted if you have to keep getting up to tend to me."

We're emotionally raw and our conversation is edgy. Gordon is worried that I want to use them for daytime, too, and he knows that isn't good for recovery. I assure him that I absolutely do not want to be sitting in wet diapers all day long and that I'm fine with using the toilet in the daytime. Eventually, we agree that using adult diapers at night, and maybe even on the airplane, is probably a good idea.

Next on the list is a waterproof sheet for the bed.

"Please don't get a rubber sheet, it would make me perspire," I ask. "I'm sure you can find the breathable waterproof sheets somewhere, maybe where you got the support belts.

They come in different sizes. I don't move around at all, so a children's bed size would be fine. Then we could use it for Finn's bed when he visits."

As a former nutritionist, I have a pretty good idea of the kind of foods I'll be eating for a while to promote healing and keep the smell of the ostomy down: low fibre, soft, non-gaseous. We're only going to be at Santa Maria for three days, so we agree that he won't bring in a large variety. We settle on duplications of my hospital diet: applesauce, bananas, fine rusks, jelly, pasta stars, Parmesan, chicken, zucchini, cooked carrots or squash, biscuits, Italian tea. And I would love some soup—chicken noodle, if possible. Rather than fresh carrots and squash, I suggest that he buy baby food. Gordon pretends to be incredulous. Is this Joyce speaking? The lover of variety, flavour, and texture? The detester of soft, bland, and mushy? Laughing, I assure him that this is all I can tolerate right now. He needs to plan two sets of meals—unless he wants to try my diet. We both know *that* isn't going to happen! (Mr. Garlic himself.)

Speaking of food, here is Claudia with a heaping plate of chicken, zucchini, and pasta stars. It looks and smells delicious. It is. Gordon watches me savour the flavours for a while and then leaves to find lunch for himself, and to shop.

Son, Daughter-in-Law, and Sister have left, too. It's just Mamma and me, alone, to have an after-lunch nap.

Until in strides a Catholic priest dressed in full vestments—white alb, cincture, and stole heavily laden with beautiful golden Or Nue embroidery at all the extremities, perfectly highlighting the simple pectoral cross with a ruby embedded in its centre.

He stands in the middle of our room, at the foot of our beds, raises his ringed hand, and intones: "*Benedictio Dei omnipotentis, Patris et Filii et Spiritus Sancti, descendant super vos, et maneat semper*. Amen."

He turns and leaves.

Mamma curses, "*Bastardo!*" and actually spits on the floor!

I wonder how the priest would have reacted if I had told him I'd already been to heaven this week.

Deciding that it is a good time to try my land legs, solo, again, I'm already sitting upright when my ostomy specialist arrives, carrying a huge parcel. Thinking it is time for another lesson, I pull the bedcovers back.

He shakes his head and nods to me. "*No. No.* You, now."

He's not here for more instruction but to deliver supplies. Opening the package, he shows me what is inside and counts it all. There are enough bags and rings for three weeks! Amazed, I thank him profusely but then gently remind him that I also need a pair of scissors. He is baffled by the word "scissors," so I pick up one of the sealing rings that have to be trimmed and use my fingers to demonstrate.

"Ah. *Forbici.*" He says he will try.

He and Gordon meet in the doorway. This is like a three-ring circus. And I don't even know anyone in Italy! Just as well Gordon did come back. I'm a little wobbly this afternoon and thankful for his steady presence as we slowly shuffle up and down the hallways. My brain is finally remembering what signals to give my feet for walking, but my feet are still so swollen they don't have a lot of feeling, making it difficult to balance.

My ankles are swollen, too, so they don't move properly. Now I know how my African students felt when I was teaching them to use the treadle sewing machine. After they'd experienced a lifetime of rigid-ankle shuffles along dirt paths, balancing heavy jugs on their heads, I had to teach them how to move their ankles to make the treadle go. Kneeling, I would place my hands on their feet and move them back and forth, back and forth. It was a motion they had never done. Now it is a motion that I cannot remember.

Gordon and I don't talk much until we're back in the room. I'm still low on oxygen and so unfit that even my slow walks are an aerobic challenge.

Once I'm settled in, Gordon tells me about his shopping experience. He is delighted. He was able to purchase everything on the list—including the adult diapers and the waterproof sheet. The support belt supplier had both items. Gordon must have had everyone in the shop in hysterics. Not knowing what size to buy, he went around hugging all the women until he found my size. Lucky women! By that time, the salesperson must have figured out that he needed adult diapers for a woman, not himself.

We're interrupted by another visitor. Dr. Lollio this time. His appearance is even more dishevelled than usual, the paper he is carrying with grave concern the likely culprit. He wants Gordon to read it over. It is a rough draft of his discharge notes, and he wants to make sure he has included all the essentials.

How fortunate that he asked. Gordon observes that a critical component for travel insurance compensation is missing: "Was the surgery essential for life, or could it have waited until returning home?" Recognizing the importance of Gordon's insight, Dr. Lollio rushes out to insert the necessary comment before passing the notes along to Dr. Bing for her input.

Tomorrow is a big day. Gordon leaves—he still has preparations to make for me back at the apartment. For the first time in twelve days, I'm sitting in my chair when my dinner arrives. More pasta stars, covered in tomato sauce, smothered with Parmesan. Delicious, but one nibble is enough. I fall asleep right where I sit.

Marta wakes me, and together we get me ready for bed. I no sooner get settled than my ostomy specialist returns. Tenderly, he introduces his shy wife, Anna Marie. She seems so pleased to meet me. He presents a small package—a new pair of scissors! I am astounded that he would go to this trouble, and thank him.

He turns, holds out his hand to his wife, and they leave, fingers intertwined. Just as they disappear into the hallway, I notice he is wearing old-fashioned trouser clips. I picture them on a bicycle, absolutely sure that she rides sidesaddle on the bar in front of him, carefully chauffeured by her gentle husband.

Smiling, I fall asleep—

To be awakened hours later by spasms of pain in my lower back. I breathe through each stab of pain, expecting relief.

"Breathe in . . . Breathe out. Breathe in relief . . . Breathe out pain. Breathe in coolness . . . Breathe out heat. Breathe in balance . . . Breathe out distress."

The pain spreads from side to side, the spasms happening more rapidly. My breathing becomes panting. My only thought: "The fluid around my lungs has returned. They're going to have to drain it again. Dear God, please, no!"

Only when a night nurse arrives do I realize I've pressed the call button. She can see the pain on my face and listens carefully as I describe it. More importantly, she watches as I clench my fist faster and faster to show how the pain is changing. She raises the head of the bed, then gently bends me forward, guiding my hands to the area of pain. With no support belt on, my back is fully exposed. She places her hands on my back, and then carefully traces where the spasms are occurring.

She settles me back onto the mattress, then calmly looks me in the eye, and says, "I'll call the doctor for some medication, to stop the pain."

"Has the fluid returned?"

"*No, no.* It is not that. The medication will stop the pain."

"I don't have to have the fluid drained again?"

"*No, no.* I'm sure."

"The medication—*no morphine.*"

She smiles, agreeing. "*No morfina.*"

My questions have come through tightly clenched teeth. The exchange has cost me. The pain is raging. My breathing is shallow. I feel like I'm going to faint. Seeing this, she hurries out.

Although it seems like hours, I know it has only been minutes when she returns, carrying a small glass of water and a small packet. She opens the packet and pours a powder into the water—it bubbles and she stirs it until there are no more bubbles. Somehow I'm able to open my mouth and gradually sip between the spasms. Miraculously, the medicine starts to work almost instantly. And I sleep.

12

OCTOBER 4

AWAKING TO morning light, I see my little feathered friend flying away with straw in her beak. As if the bird senses that I am finally awake, she flies back, pecks the window, fluffs her feathers, and flies away again. I am left alone. I think she just said goodbye.

Today, I am to leave this place. Strangely, I'm sad. I'm also a little afraid. This has been my cocoon, the womb that saved my life. Am I really well enough to leave? Is it fair to place the responsibility of my care on Gordon's shoulders? How will we cope?

The day nurse Salvadore notices my wet cheeks when he comes in to check on me. His warm, liquid caramel eyes exude empathy. His deep baritone voice caresses me as he says, "*Bravissima,*" over and over. It is like a lullaby.

When I'm calm, he gives me a packet of the pain medication the night nurse gave me last night. I'm to take it at bedtime. He very carefully tells me to use only half the packet in a small glass of water and let the bubbly liquid get flat before taking it. He motions to me that if I drink it while it's bubbly, my ostomy will make strange noises. The sounds he makes are hilarious. Our laughter cheers us both.

He leaves and then returns almost immediately. Sheepishly, he gives me a whole boxful of the same medication. He shrugs his shoulders: "*Di riserva.*" I take that to mean, "Just in case." He is so thoughtful.

In rushes Dr. Lollio, white lab coat flapping behind him. He tells me he has to do an emergency surgery, but when he's finished he'll be back with my discharge papers and to say goodbye. He has brought anticoagulant for my trip home and explains that I need it to prevent blood clots from forming during our long flight. They're a danger for anyone with poor circulation but especially for people who don't move much during the flight. When he learns that our trip includes an overnight in Frankfurt, his chin falls to his chest for a moment as he thinks, and then he tells me to use it just before the long flight home, that I don't need it between Florence and Frankfurt. With that, he practically runs out of the room to the emergency that awaits him.

As planned, Gordon arrives late morning. He wanted to make sure our apartment was ready for me. Since housekeeping isn't part of our rental fee, I think he had some serious cleanup to do—he certainly hasn't had much time to do anything other than care for me.

He's brought some choices of clothes. We struggle to get them on. Even though I've probably lost twenty-five or thirty pounds, not much goes over the bandages and the ostomy. Everything feels uncomfortable. This makes me pretty grumpy. I try to hide it, but we both know. What makes it worse is that I know I should be so grateful to be alive, but I'm pissed off that this has happened to me, and I'm even more pissed off that any positive self-image I ever had has been destroyed. I am sore, I am ugly, and I am miserable. What a great way to journey home with the person who has shown nothing but absolute love, acceptance, and devotion.

Waiting is beyond tedious. Dr. Lollio's emergency surgery must be very complicated. Gordon leaves to get some lunch. Fortunately, I'm not hungry, because the roast beef on my plate looks like leather. The zucchini might be left over from yesterday; one bite is enough.

I miss my feathered friend. She hasn't returned. My tears do, though.

A chapel door must have opened. For a brief moment, I hear an organ—a sombre chord played in tremolo—I think it is in E-flat minor. Perfect for my mood.

What an experience I have had. Who will ever believe me? An evangelical preacher; a fortune teller; a Hassidic Jew hired by a Roma to say the Kaddish, the prayer for the dead, at her funeral; sorcery; lost souls; my own sublime moment at the threshold of the next life. Even the expected experience—a blessing from a Catholic priest in an Italian hospital— blasphemed by a little old lady in the bed next to me. No. No one will ever believe me.

Marta startles me out of my reverie as she draws the privacy curtains along their tracks. She's here to change my bandage one last time before I leave. She gently cleans the incision under the zipper of metal staples.

A couple of catgut stitches are starting to pull where the initial laparoscopic work was done. Tiny little incisions. Great long threads of wiry suture. They rub against everything, and even though there are only a half dozen stitches, they are driving me crazy. Marta won't take them out, though.

"*Piu tardo*," she says, which I gather means "later."

As she is doing her work, she is carefully showing me how I must look after myself. She bustles out and returns with a box filled with sterile cotton, bandages, and a small bottle of sterile water for cleaning. Once more, the staff are making sure that they continue to care for me even after I am discharged.

In Canada, do we care for our foreign hospital patients with as much humanity? I can only hope so.

Soon after Gordon returns from lunch, Dr. Lollio brings his final letter for the insurance company, says goodbye to me, and asks Gordon to come to the office for the last details of my discharge.

Dr. Bing comes in to say goodbye. Amazing. Both surgeons who saved my life thirteen days ago have come to wish us well. Gordon tells her that he doesn't know where to pick me up. Dr. Bing offers to wheel me down to the Emergency entrance, where she will arrange for Gordon to park.

She settles me into a wheelchair and then passes me my beautiful basket of mauve orchids and still-lovely single red rose. I am covered in flowers and feel like a strange mix of bride and corpse. Dr. Bing laughs when I tell her.

We meet as planned at the Emergency entrance. Everything seems good until I have to get into the car. I have no idea how to do it. I can't bend. I can't lift my legs. I don't even remember how to get into a car. I stand there, wobbling uncertainly from one foot to the other.

Seeing my predicament, Dr. Bing helps me turn my back to the car, right at the front passenger seat. She and Gordon support me as I move my bum down to the edge of the car seat. The metal sutures screech at me. I have no flexibility, no ability to lift my feet or swing my body around. Gordon and Dr. Bing have to do it all.

Thank God our rented Peugeot wagon is large for Italy. Thank God the seats are slippery leather. The seat belt is snapped around me—my hands holding it away from my body and its new appendage. With a lovely smile, Dr. Bing closes my door and then waves before she turns away, pushing the empty wheelchair.

We are alone.

For a moment we sit in silence, not quite believing.

Gordon reaches over and brushes his fingers along my cheek. "Care to go home?" he asks softly.

I turn away, overwhelmed by the fear of leaving the secure womb of the hospital and its staff. Within its cloisters, my recovery seemed miraculous and nearly complete. But the previously simple, now agonizingly complex act of getting into the car has laid reality bare—I am an oozing slab of flesh as dependent as a newborn. The euphoria of being discharged is gone. My confidence is shattered, my fear for Gordon's responsibility appalling in its scope.

As we drive through the streets of Empoli, Gordon gives a running monologue of the places we pass—the wee flower shop where he bought the rose I'm holding, the pharmacy with automatic pill dispensing, the mall where he purchased my nighties and our precious business-class air tickets home. From the highway, I realize that during our first exploration of Tuscany fourteen days earlier, we had passed Empoli—I recognize a building and ask what he thinks it is.

"I don't think. I know. That's the mall—just from a different angle."

A few moments later, we exit the highway, beginning our winding journey along ever-narrowing country roads that often intersect with roundabouts. He has become an Italian driver, negotiating the tricky traffic circles with confidence.

Our silence, our love of driving together, the golden Tuscan light of late afternoon are soothing. Over and over, I breathe in that comfort, and breathe out the pain and the feeling of helplessness.

We stop once, at the small grocery store in Mura to buy some bananas for me. I stay in the car, isolated. Panic sets in, but the warmth of the sun through the window helps. Across the street I see a red cross. It, too, is comforting, though I have no idea whether it identifies a pharmacy or a doctor's office or a medical clinic. For me, it is a reassuring symbol.

We continue our journey back to our Tuscan farmhouse apartment. Within moments, we pass the narrow driveway to Masa, the restaurant where we had planned to celebrate our twenty-fifth anniversary—surrounded by vineyards, enjoying local wines and an exquisite meal prepared by the renowned chef. Now across the rickety wooden bridge, and then a sharp turn to the left, past the centuries-old brick church still being used by its parishioners, past the local trattoria and bakery where we ate fourteen nights ago, past the vineyard where wild boar are hunted—to the black iron gates of Santa Maria. The gates swing open without Gordon entering the code—Stefania and her father, Giuseppe, are waiting for us. Respecting our privacy, they don't bustle over to help. They have already arranged for Gordon to drive directly to our apartment—a privilege.

And now it is time to get out of the car. How are we going to accomplish this? When we work together in small, awkward places, tempers usually flare—not something either of us needs today. As I'm struggling with what directions to give him, Gordon reaches across and unbuckles the seat belt, while carefully holding the buckle so that it doesn't snap across my tender abdomen. He slips his hands underneath me and lifts me out of the car. I have no idea how he does this without seriously injuring his back. He turns, slips one hand onto my back, lowers me so that my feet touch the ground, and then holds me in place until I feel steady enough to move. It is our first embrace in fourteen days.

He is my prop as I slowly shuffle along the flagstone path to our ground-floor apartment. Even the two steps up to the door are an incomprehensible challenge. My brain and my muscles are simply not functioning together. In the end, Gordon carries me up. On the porch are a table and chairs. Stefania has put a cushion on one of the chairs and on the table a vase of flowers from the garden—Tuscan sunflowers. Beside the vase, a simple note: "Welcome back, Mrs. Joyce."

Our plan was to get me to the bedroom for a nap, but I can't take another step. Awkwardly, I settle into the cushioned chair. Gordon brings a wastepaper basket, turns it upside down, and props my feet up. That doesn't work—even with the support belt—I just start to slide off the chair. His alternative? Use another chair as a footstool. Better.

Despite the autumn warmth, I am shivering. My gentle husband brings a blanket and cocoons me inside it. He leaves again.

Alone. Breathing in fresh air laden with the perfume of the sun-warmed roses in the garden just steps from me. Oh, to bury my nose in those beauties! For now, I sit and drink in the rich layers of their fragrance and their robust colours.

Gordon slides into my vision. In his hand, a cup of tea. The golden nectar with hints of honey that I've come to enjoy. On a plate, buttery tea biscuits, similar to the ones in the hospital. Comfort foods. Several sips later, with the biscuits untouched, I nod off.

The sound of people returning from their tourist adventures rouses me. The day is moving toward evening and I have yet to have the shower that I had promised myself. I am so looking forward to washing my hair, getting really clean. Marta told me that I don't have to worry about getting the incision or the ileostomy wet. This is going to be bliss!

Once we get to the bathroom, we talk about how to get everything I need into the right places. One of the plastic deck chairs just fits into the shower stall so that I don't have to stand. We put a hand towel on the seat so that it isn't cold, and so that it isn't slippery.

Although I desperately want privacy, it is soon obvious that I cannot undress myself. For the first time in almost thirty years, I'm ashamed of my nakedness in front of Gordon—my body feels raw and desperately ugly. It isn't just the incision and the bag. After surgery and thirteen days of total inactivity, all my muscle is jelly, the pull of gravity from illness and aging now drooping my entire frame and its skin. I can't look at him directly, I'm so worried that I will see disgust in his eyes.

Although the bag is almost full, I figure I have enough time to shower before it absolutely has to be changed. Gordon settles me into the shower stall, gets the water running, rigs up a way for me to access the handheld shower, and leaves.

As the steam rises, I sit for a moment, enjoying the moisture. But the experience of showering, of washing my hair, is soon frustration personified. The incision shrieks at me when I lift my arm to raise the shower head over my hair. I'm lucky to even dampen my hair. Squeezing the shampoo out of the travel bottle is my next challenge. I have no grip strength at all. I stick it between my knees and squeeze, using my hands to shove my knees together. It shoots its contents straight up and then down onto the shower stall floor, out of my reach. A few drops of shampoo land on my thighs. The sudsy lather I had imagined is nothing more than a paltry lubrication. The brisk scalp scrubbing I'd anticipated giving myself is a half-hearted rub. Yet within a split second, my heart is pounding, my head spinning. How could washing my hair be so much work?

I look down, and there, collecting onto the adhesive edges of my enormous bandage is a thick pile of my hair that has fallen out. With no defences left, I weep until the water runs cold.

Concerned at how long I'm taking, Gordon slips in to check on me. Seeing my distress, he turns off the water and dries me.

Now it's time to change the bandage, and change the bag. I decide to get rid of the wet bandage first. The loose hairs have worked their way under the bandage and into the incision under the metal sutures. One by one, I have to pull the hairs out. By the time I'm finished, my hands are shaking. Removing the bandage from its package and getting it in the right place is almost impossible, but it's good enough.

Next step—replace the now-full bag. I get it unlatched from the ring okay, but then I drop it onto the floor. Foul-smelling liquid splatters everywhere—on the floor, on the toilet, up the walls, up my legs, even onto my face. Not thinking, I try to lean over to pick up the bag. Out of my uncovered hole spurts more of the stuff—this time warm, and it soils the ring that I was hoping not to have to clean.

ARRGHHHH!! is what I want to scream, but my throat is still raw, my vocal cords letting out nothing more than a raspy squawk. Even so, Gordon hears and pokes his frightened face around the door. All I can do is apologize for the frightful mess that he's going to have to clean up. I don't know how he's going to do it without vomiting, the smell is so overpowering.

But first, I have to get the fresh bag on. This time, I remember to cover the hole with toilet paper to capture its constant emissions. The ring cleans up okay, but my shaking fingers have a hell of a time locking the bag in place. In the end, Gordon has to do that, too, stepping around all the mess on the floor.

And then we realize that not only do I need to get washed again, but the bandage also has to be replaced—it got spattered, too. From somewhere deep inside of me comes a cold rage of sheer determination. I rip the bandage off and repeat the careful cleaning process. By the time I'm finished, Gordon has heated some water in a pot for a sponge bath. While I'm cleaning myself up, he tackles the floor.

I can't take any more today. I want to go to bed. I need to escape.

He's put the waterproof mattress protector under the bottom sheet and a towel on top of the bottom sheet, just as we planned. I ask him to put a diaper on me so that if I fall asleep, he doesn't need to wake me. As exhausted as we both are, we do have a few giggles about this.

Just as he's leaving the room, he asks "Would you like some music?"

Ohhhh—a lovely idea.

Knowing that I'm not going to want to wear earbuds, he sets my iPad on a table, selects my Bocelli playlist, gets the volume just right, and leaves me to enjoy. The beautiful tenor voice soothes my soul, and I relax. As the last notes of "L'Ultimo Re" fade, it is twilight. I am still, and on the verge of that liminal space that has been my home.

I think about Philip and the beautiful memorial service that was held in his honour. Philip loved a good party. He loved choral music. Raised in a British boarding school, he appreciated eloquence. He loved his family life. His memorial service was a reflection of who he was and how he will be remembered.

What would I like to happen at a memorial service for me? I would like to share who I was—from my perspective—and the lessons I have learned, the joys I have had, how I have lived my life. The images begin to flow.

As a serious, very shy, beautiful six-year-old girl with long blond ringlets, concerned I had not learned to print my name but so proud when the church's old janitor taught me, and then devastated when my eldest brother gleefully told me the word I had printed was "pig." A sad introduction to the abuses adults impose on children, and an early lesson about vulnerability. At six, I became an advocate for children, forevermore.

The family Sunday dinner table where people from away were welcomed, their stories heard. Teenagers from Kingcome Inlet, Alert Bay, and Bella Coola. Theological students and ordained ministers from Nigeria and Japan. Friends of my father sharing their experiences as prison and hospital chaplains. My godfather, also my father's bishop. My imagination was fired by their stories. News and events from the world would be more than facts; they would be about the humanity and the goodness of the people involved, forevermore.

The smell, the heat, the sounds, the pulse of Mother Africa, seducing me for two years with the harsh simplicity of sheer existence. In my memorial I would have a slideshow of the herds of giraffe, zebra, gazelle, elephant, buffalo that are vivid memories. The lions sprawling on their perch in a thorn tree. The flock of flamingos taking wing and forming a pink cloud over Lake Manyara. The smell of gourds filled with raw milk and urine carried by the Masai warriors on the rickety bus on the dusty dirt road to Moshi. And in the background would be Mozart's Concerto for Clarinet in A— the producers of *Out of Africa* got it right; it is the perfect counterpoint of lonely clarity to emphasize the majesty of this earth's womb of life. But then the background music would switch to the umpteen-part African harmony like that of the Msalato schoolgirls making staid British hymns come alive, or the music of the Young Swimmers singing "The Lion

Sleeps Tonight"—a song they were singing long before it was discovered by the Nylons. Mother Africa grounded me, forevermore.

As a nineteen-year-old bride, I discovered on my wedding night that I had made a sad mistake. Believing the "you made your bed, you lie in it" cultural norm of the times, I remained in that ill-matched marriage for seventeen years. Each painful experience, though, deepened my inner strength and opened me to excel beyond anything I could have expected. And the marriage provided penultimate blessings—two daughters I have cherished from the moment they were conceived, and will, forevermore.

Another blessing came later—the deep love of a good and generous man. Gordon found the woman in me, and adored that person he discovered. I returned his adoration, all the more able to enter fully into our profoundly mature relationship because of the lessons I learned earlier. It was not always easy, but together we continued to learn about relationships between man and woman—the importance of trust, honesty, and consideration—lessons that have enriched our lives, and are there for everyone to learn, forevermore.

The awakening, the quickening, the deepening, the understanding of the capacity for love—this has been the foundation of my life. It has been expressed most obviously in love for my grandchildren, but I have felt it deeply for friends, family, all people known and unknown. This is what I would like to be remembered for—my love.

At the end of my memorial, I would like these words read, from me to those I leave behind:

"The final music of my memorial is Bocelli's 'L'Incontro' with Bono reading the introductory poem. It is the finest expression of the depth of love I have ever heard. Although it is about a man's love for his newborn son, it is truly how I feel about all of you. You'll hear it now and because I would like it to stay with you for a while, I have a request of you. Once the song is ended, please leave this place and me in silence, not speaking until the doors are closed and we have truly parted. May this song remind you of the love I have for you—now, and forevermore."

I feel the tears on my face. They are tears of peace, of satisfaction in my life, well spent, of knowing that the love that I feel will be expressed, and that it is fine for me to leave. I am aware that I am holding shimmering scissors in my hand. Yes, I can sever the silver thread that is my bond to this earthly existence.

As I reach up to sever the thread, Philip appears. He isn't as clear as before, but perhaps that is because he's at the head of a brilliant tunnel of white light.

"You daft silly, what's the point of preparing that beautiful memorial service if you don't tell anyone about it?" he says. Although neither of us is in our physical bodies, I feel the warmth of a touch. "Besides, you have a promise to keep, don't you?"

He is gone. I am alone, still gazing at the silver thread. Then I realize I no longer have the shimmering scissors. They have disappeared.

Sighing, I focus on my surroundings. It is nighttime. The frogs have begun their serenade.

Gordon tiptoes into the room. He pauses beside me, and then quietly makes his way to the twin-size cot across the room, beneath the open window. Its creaking beneath his weight joins the croaking of the frogs.

I wake to an unfamiliar feeling—a warm sliminess spreading across my abdomen. It takes me a moment to realize that, once again, I am covered in liquid feces. The bag must have come unfastened. I am frantic this will wreck the bedding, maybe even the mattress, until I remember all the precautions we have taken. Getting my breathing under control, I use my mind to investigate the sensation.

The diaper covers the bag, but is the mess being contained? Yes, it is. Good.

Gordon is sleeping so soundly, I don't want to wake him, and without his hearing aids, I doubt that I could, unless I threw something at him. That's a joke—I have lousy aim even at the best of times. Whatever I threw would either break or fly soundlessly right out the window.

"This is not an emergency. It can be cleaned up in the morning. Let him sleep," I decide, before falling back to sleep myself.

13

OCTOBER 5

THERE'S NOT a glimmer of morning light, but the rooster in the neighbour's yard proudly announces the beginning of a new day. Sure of himself, he issues only one "Cock-a-doodle-doo!" Out of respect for his prowess, there is a moment of silence, and then a chorus of birdsong responds from the trees—a gradual crescendo beginning with the soft throb of a mourning dove, joined by the cheeky conversations of chickadees, and climaxing with joyful melodies from two robins calling to one another, one from the tree just outside our window.

The morning announced, once again there is silence. Dawn's first light appears.

BOOM! BOOM! BOOM! The sound of rifle shots ricochets off the hills. Running feet. Deep shouts. The wild boar hunt is on in these Tuscan hills.

Gordon wakes, stretches, and then looks over at me, a smile on his face, happy to see me. He walks over and bends for a kiss. We both enjoy the renewal of our morning ritual, but he wrinkles his nose as he stands upright again.

"Guess there's some cleanup to do?" he asks.

All I can do is nod.

Without another word, he assembles the necessary supplies for a sponge bath. There's no point in getting me up—I have to wear the support belt to move, and that's not going to happen until I'm clean.

When he peels back the covers, we are both so grateful for all the protection he had put in place. The mess has oozed onto the towels but not onto the bedding. The towels are ours—Gordon purchased them just yesterday.

Although the ostomy specialist had assured me that the bags could not burst, this one must have been faulty, because it definitely has a leak. The good news is that we don't have to change the beeswax attachment ring that I had to replace yesterday. That would have been painful—it's a strong adhesive, especially when fresh, and the skin underneath was raw yesterday. But the bandage has to be changed again, and the skin underneath it is getting raw as well.

As soon as I'm clean, I'm anxious to get up. I need to build strength and stamina for the trip home three days from now. Gordon wraps the support belt around me. It is inside out. We are both frustrated. But he's successful the second time.

He reaches down to lift me into sitting position. Something goes wrong in my back. I ignore it and ask him to hurry—to get my feet swung over the edge of the bed so that I am sitting fully upright. The strange sensation batters me, quick shocks of pain pelting from the inside, all over my back, like fiery-hot hailstones hurtling under my skin, bouncing around to be followed over and over by others, unending. Any movement at all provokes the storm. I cannot move. Not a muscle. My breathing is limited to shallow, short sips of air.

We are both engulfed in fear. What is happening? What should we do?

I wonder if the spasms I had in my lower back the night before last were a prelude to this. The drugs the night nurse gave me sure had an immediate effect. How am I going to explain to Gordon what to do? I can barely breathe. It's an effort to make any sound at all, my throat is still so raw. As I'm mulling all this over, he goes to the bathroom and quickly returns with one of the packets Salvadore provided. Oh—that's right, when he was unpacking my stuff from the hospital, he asked about that package and I told him about my back pains.

He checks to see if I want it. I'm to blink once if I do.

Yes.

He checks to make sure he knows how to prepare it—half of the packet in a small glass of water and stir until there are no more bubbles?

I blink again. Yes.

He hurries away to prepare it, while I wonder how I'm going to drink it without going into total spasm.

The glass he is holding when he returns has a straw in it—something he bought "just in case." The thanks in my eyes ease the worry from his face for a moment. I sip and swallow. It takes a long time for me to finish, even though there is only half a cup of liquid. Every motion is measured and slow.

I'm getting tired sitting on the edge of the bed and fluid is starting to puff up my feet. There isn't much we can do—just wait for the medication to kick in. Gordon stands in front of me, ready to catch me should I fall, but he doesn't try to hold me in place for fear of making things worse.

Gradually, gradually, the spasms lessen. They don't disappear, but the rapid-fire is slower, and the intensity of the pain drops from a nine to a five—bearable enough to try to move. With Gordon's help, I stand. I nearly collapse from a whole new round of pain. We stand together, waiting for it to pass. After five minutes or so, I realize I need to pee. Oh God, how am I going to walk to the bathroom, let alone sit on the toilet? But it has to be done. It takes every ounce of grit that I have.

Now what? There is no way I'm going to lie down again, but the apartment is claustrophobic. I need fresh air. The chair on the veranda is calling me. That's where I settle.

It is now well past noon. I've had no food for more than twenty-four hours; Gordon has had neither breakfast nor lunch. The only exercise I've had has been to hold myself rigid for hours. The laundry Gordon had planned to get done is in a heap on the floor. We are forced to live in the moment.

Both exhausted, we sit for a while, silent together. Eventually, Gordon leaves to prepare some food for us. He offers to feed me, but the food he's brought is soft and I'm able to move my arm enough to feed myself—a peeled banana, some applesauce, and some yogourt. I can only eat half of it.

His meal is much more interesting. He loves his breakfasts in Italy—thinly sliced meats and cheeses, a hard-boiled egg, fresh crusty bread with local jam, a mix of berries. Strawberries, blackberries, and raspberries today.

The tea he made for me has cooled enough to drink, but I can't lift the cup. He spoons it to my lips.

The laundry has to be done now or the towels won't be dry for my bed tonight—Mother Nature does the drying here. I assure him that I'll be fine; after all, he'll just be next door.

But long before he comes back, the spasms return in full force. He doesn't ask—my rigid agony must be very, very evident. Quickly, he gets another packet of the medication and tells me that he's going to ask Stefania to translate the directions for him. Maybe I can have a stronger dose, or take it more frequently. I decide that it doesn't matter what the instructions say; I'm going to take as much as I need to get these spasms under control.

"You can take a full packet up to six times per day, so that's every four hours. It hasn't been four hours, but who cares?" Gordon says.

He prepares it and patiently holds the glass for me to sip and swallow. Then he sits with me, waiting for it to take effect. He ignores my suggestion that I'll be fine on my own.

"We don't know if a double dose will knock you out. I'd rather be here with you."

The double dose works! Like a miracle, within minutes the spasms ease, and then disappear. I can breathe! Cautiously, I adjust my position in the chair. I can move!

Visitors come through the garden. Little Clara was born just days before we arrived at Santa Maria. She is Stefania's daughter and I have been longing to meet her. Oh my, she is gorgeous. Just a month old, she's holding her head upright, her round dark eyes curiously exploring from the security of her father's arms. She hears my voice, probably hears my wistfulness that I am not able to hold her, and responds with a soft grunt as if to tell me she understands.

Her father, Matteo, asks when we are leaving for home. When he learns that we will pack on Sunday and leave on Monday, he is disappointed. He explains that this Sunday is Clara's christening; it will be a very special day for everyone.

They stay for a while longer and I can tell that he wants to ask me something. Eventually, he gets up his courage.

"How was the hospital care?" he asks anxiously.

"It was outstanding. The hospital was spotless. The staff were wonderful caregivers and highly professional. I couldn't have asked for more. You seem concerned. Why?"

"Well, you know, there is talk about how some hospitals are mismanaged, so I was wondering if you had any problems."

"None. I only hope our health care in Canada is as good as what I received here."

As they leave, he turns and promises that they will come back for another visit tomorrow. With a smile and a wave, proud papa and baby say, "*Ciao*."

Gordon is finishing the laundry. I know that when he comes back he's going to want me to get some exercise. He's right. That long trip home is looming, and, since leaving the hospital, my strength has probably diminished, not improved. But—oh—I am so, so very exhausted; the thought of walking is overwhelming.

Sure enough, he comes back looking worried and determined.

"We need to get you walking. I'll fix up the bed, and then I'm coming out to get you on your feet. I know you're not feeling up to it, but if you don't, I don't know how you'll make it home."

When he gets me onto my swollen feet, my legs give way. He catches me, holding me upright. Then we slowly, carefully walk along the thirty-foot-long veranda and back. He wants me to go down the steps and into the garden, but I refuse. Instead, we walk back and forth on the smooth tile of the veranda. After the fourth trip, I beg to stop. We negotiate. I can stop, but we need to repeat this again after supper, preferably going into the garden.

Our neighbours return from their day's exploration. They are delighted to see me, to see that I truly did survive. They have been very kind—inviting Gordon for supper one night and sharing drinks with him last night while I was listening to Bocelli. Their concern for us is a reminder of the essential kindness of humanity. The instant that disaster strikes, we reach out to those affected, no matter who or where they are. Tornadoes. Hurricanes. Fires. Earthquakes. Tsunamis. Cancer. Accidents. I wonder why we are so slow to respond to human-imposed disasters, like genocide. Is it because we are loath to be reminded of the darker side of our human nature?

The smell of garlic simmering in olive oil is a signal for them to leave us in privacy. The timing is perfect. Within moments, Gordon brings out two plates of pasta. Mine is a heaping mound of pasta stars in a light tomato sauce. His is spaghettini with garlic and hot red pepper flakes lightly browned in lots of olive oil. Both plates of pasta are covered with freshly grated Parmesan. Although his looks delicious, and I hope he makes it for me sometime, the simplicity of mine is perfect. It's easy to eat with a spoon. The tomato sauce tastes light and fresh. The cheese is enough protein to keep me satiated.

We linger on the veranda for a while. Just as I'm about to suggest that it's time for bed, Gordon reminds me of our agreement. I don't have the energy to argue, and besides, I know he's right. So we clumsily get me back on my feet and shuffle over to the edge of the veranda. It's only two shallow steps down to the garden path, but it is daunting. Even with Gordon's strong supporting arm around me, I can't figure out how to step down. Only with his patient coaxing and my absolute faith in his strength do we make it down. I wonder if I'll ever be able to manage steps on my own again.

My dark spirits soon brighten from being so close to the roses. The path meanders around them. A hint of humidity has touched these sun-warmed beauties, releasing their fragrance into the evening air. I drink in their scent. It is delicious. Quietly, we stand in their midst, Gordon's arms wrapped around me. Together, we are home.

Gradually, we make our way back to the steps. Yesterday, he had to carry me up. Today, with a lot of strong support from him, I'm able to make it up—a small victory to end the day.

Getting ready for bed is a little easier, too—no accidents in the bathroom, the pain medication a part of our routine, better coordination between us getting me into bed and un-wrapped from the support belt. Closing the door behind him,

Gordon leaves me to my thoughts; he has emails to send to family and friends, to tell of my progress today.

My favourite James Ehnes album is playing. One day, I'd love to hear him play live. I'm sure he is in love with his violin. My father always used to say, "You can't love inanimate objects." Maybe James's violin isn't inanimate?

I feel myself drifting into that liminal space again. I don't want to go there. I'm not sure I can get back again if I go there tonight. That beautiful shimmering light on the other side is so alluring. I'm already yearning for it. Last night, when I had those scissors, it would have been so right, so natural to have snipped the silver thread that keeps me here. I don't need scissors, though. I know how to break it. Tonight, if I go, I know I won't come back. But I have to keep my promise to Philip. He needs Marnie to hear his message. I'm the one he's chosen to tell it. I have to honour my promise.

I need to stay here. What can I do to make that happen? I need to keep my brain active.

I know! The first difficult question that comes to mind, I'll try to solve. I usually try to avoid those kinds of questions when I'm lying in bed, but tonight I need one. I need something that will make me think, to keep me on this side.

It doesn't take long. The question has been in my mind for ten years. We were on the train from Delhi to Jaipur. Gordon had the window seat, I had the middle seat, and a woman sat next to me in the aisle seat. We shared our fresh-roasted, spicy cashews with her, and the nibbling led to talking, first about where we were from, then about our families, then about our occupations, then about world events. Her name was Sohan. She was from the Punjab region, very fluent in English, and clearly well educated. The rapport we established was evident from her willingness to ask a probing question: "What aspirations can children in Canada possibly have?"

I asked her to unpack her question for me. I needed to understand her perspective before I could respond.

"Although India has a rapidly growing middle class, many, many children still are born into poverty and remain there. Aspirations they have are for the basics—food, water, shelter, clothing, and, if they're lucky, some education. Even the middle-class children are reminded by their parents that they are not far removed from poverty, so there remains an awareness of the importance of the basics, along with the expectation that they must study hard to improve the lot of their families. But from what I hear about Canada, there is plenty of food, water, shelter, education, and opportunity. The children seem to have everything. So, I wonder, what aspirations can children in Canada possibly have?"

Just as I was about to dig a little deeper, she realized that the next stop was Alwar, her destination. She rushed to collect her belongings. There was no more time for us.

Her question has haunted me all this time. Why? It could have been easy to dismiss; after all, once humans have their basic needs met, social, emotional, spiritual, cultural, and intellectual needs are in abundance, with plenty of room for aspiration.

I would have loved to have had a deeper conversation about that, to gain greater insight from her. Instead, her question has provoked me to observe children and families with new eyes, trying to understand more fully what helps children thrive with aspiration. I'm very grateful to Sohan for pushing me to look deeper, to look harder, and, where I can, to help.

What has been reinforced for me is that strong communities support families and children in helping them define and reach their aspirations. Being surrounded by people who care about you means that there are connections and interconnections that act as bridges sometimes, security nets sometimes, and launching trampolines sometimes. As the world is unfolding, families cannot provide all of these, and it is up to all of us to build strong communities to contribute to the well-being of children.

Communities are a bundle of social relationships. Like all relationships, they take work. They don't just happen. From what I've observed, strong communities have a commonly held vision. The vision recognizes the community as a caring, supportive network, and it has a sense of purpose. Strong communities also root their actions in a strong set of values that guide action in every undertaking, values such as the following:

Respect. Beyond tolerance, an openness to other people's wisdom and ideas, and respect for those who voice them.

Creativity. Creativity in finding ways to achieve goals, using obstacles as springboards to solutions.

Prudence. Prudence in the use of resources—a careful balancing of money, people, the environment.

Joyfulness. Delight in celebrating the aspirations, achievements, and talents of all people, especially children.

It would be wonderful to know that every child in Canada—no, the world—was embraced within caring communities, deeply committed to helping each child thrive.

Wouldn't that be something?

I'm smiling when Gordon comes in to go to bed. He smiles back. His steps seem lighter as he makes his way across the room.

I'm not afraid to close my eyes. I'm ready for a future. In my community work, I'm going to involve more children. It's time I did more to make sure their voices are heard.

14

OCTOBER 6

IT DOESN'T seem possible that it is time for the rooster to announce the coming dawn. But he does. And that is the end of any sleep. Although the songbirds offer lovely, soothing solos, the wild boar hunt, with barking dogs and booming guns, is hardly restful. We decide to begin our day as well.

Gordon is getting skilled at removing my soggy diaper and wrapping me in the support belt. But we have forgotten something and are reminded as soon as I am sitting upright—the muscle spasms in my back are immediately brutal, making even the shallowest of breaths cruelly painful. No words are needed. Gordon leaves me in my precarious position, sitting on the edge of the bed, gripping the mattress. He returns, stirring the medication vigorously, but the fizzing seems to take forever to stop.

Finally, it is ready, but I still sip it slowly so as not to choke. Swallowing is difficult when one can barely breathe.

Yesterday, we learned that if I took the medication every four hours the spasms could be controlled. Today, we learn that once they get started, it takes a long time for them to calm down. I've been sitting on the edge of the bed for more than an hour and I'm only now starting to breathe more normally.

Like it or not, I have to get moving. Monday, we begin our trip home. Right now, I'm not sure I can even sit upright in the car, let alone on a plane for hours.

It takes me hours to do the simplest of tasks—eat, brush my teeth, wash my face. It isn't just the unfamiliar tasks of caring for the incision and a completely different personal hygiene routine. I seem to have lost the memory of how to do any of it. Nothing is by rote. No task, no movement comes naturally—including coordination. I drop things. I bump against things. I bite my tongue. I hit my gums with my toothbrush, making my gums bleed. I cannot reach high enough to brush my hair. By the time I'm finished, I'm soaked with sweat, breathing shallowly to control the muscle spasms that are starting again. It is time for more medication.

When Gordon prepares it in the kitchen, he realizes that we don't have enough to get me home. He gives me the glass and then leaves. When he comes back, he tells me that he's been talking to Laura. She's told him where there is a pharmacy, and also where he might be able to get a couple of duffle bags for all our stuff. I understand why we need a pharmacy, but not why we need duffle bags.

"We came with a small suitcase each. They were both full. We each carried on a backpack. They were both full. With all your supplies, and the things we bought in Paris and here, we need extra luggage. The good news is that since we're going business class, we won't be paying extra," Gordon explains.

"I'm hoping that you'll come with me today. The drive will show us whether you can cope Monday. If we have to postpone our trip, we will."

Then, with a grin, he adds, "Oh—and if you are willing to walk halfway to where the car is parked, I'll reward you with a lemon gelato! Laura says there's a really good gelato shop right across from the luggage place."

He knows me well. There's not a chance we're going to postpone our trip home. And the thought of leaving Italy without another lemon gelato is too much. So I agree, but not before I ask him to take the orchids to Laura to give to Clara for her christening tomorrow.

As we shuffle slowly along the path in front of the office, Laura comes out to thank me, saying, "I know that Mamma will have them in the centre of the table. I wish you could be there."

I can just imagine a huge gathering of family and friends, celebrating Clara's christening with food, wine, toasts, love, song, laughter... and my orchids. It feels nice to be a part of it. I'm sure my dear community foundation friends back on Bowen would approve of how I have extended their love and their gift to Clara and her family.

Filled with this feeling, we walk all the way to the car. Before I ponder how to get in, Gordon picks me up and places me inside, then carefully buckles me in. I am so grateful, and close to tears of exhaustion—yet again.

We drive along the winding country roads and I am struck by the need to return to Italy for the vacation we had planned. This is just what I had imagined. The early October sun is warming the fields with its golden light, creating blue ground mist that dances briefly, then vanishes before it reaches the horizon. The deep blue grapes are hanging ponderously, filled with lusciousness to be harvested with thanks, and then savoured.

We pass through a village—Corazzano. A tight cluster of narrow houses, some rust-coloured brick, some soft, mustard-coloured, smooth plaster. There are no sidewalks. The front porches come right out to the road, and on many of them are people sitting in single rows, holding glasses of wine or tiny cups of espresso. Old women in black, faces open, wrinkled, and serene, hair held captive by sombre head scarves tied severely in place. Old men in dark olive pants with wide suspenders holding their striped shirts in place, sleeves rolled up to reveal muscular, sun-browned arms. The delight that spreads across faces as a toddler runs from a doorway and heads along a porch calling out to one of them. I want to imprint this scene on my mind. The comfort of tradition. The comfort of home. The seductive charm of Tuscany.

As we pass, Gordon waves to them. The gentle faces relax into deep, toothless smiles, and his wave is returned. I feel as if we have been blessed.

We pass it before the sign registers its meaning with Gordon. The pharmacy. We've only gone past fifty feet or so. The road is a little wider here, so he pulls over and parks in front of a house. He leaves the keys in the car and gets out. I notice a sign: *"Parcheggio Residente."* It must mean resident parking. There is no way I can catch Gordon's attention. I can't open the door; I can't shout; I can't twist; I can't wave. I'm trapped in this useless, helpless body.

Just then, in the side mirror, I see an army-style truck pulling in behind us, blocking the driveway of the house. I hear big dogs barking. The driver gets out. He's wearing camouflage hunting gear. A wild boar hunter. For sure he's got a shotgun or a rifle or something in his truck.

"Oh no. He's looking annoyed. He's walking toward our car. What am I going to do?" I think.

My imagination takes hold. "The keys are in the ignition. I can't reach them. I might be kidnapped. I might be killed. No one would know where I am."

Before he reaches the driver's door, he turns around, cursing. He opens the black iron gateway, goes to the back of the truck, and lets out two enormous, howling black dogs. They're on leashes. There must be food waiting for them—they rush through the gate, waiting impatiently while their owner latches it closed.

Gordon misses the whole episode, and is surprised to be so happily welcomed back. After I explain why I want us to get out of there, though he understands my anxiety, he insists on telling me all about the pharmacist and his helpfulness before he starts the car and drives away. After all, he needs to share his success story. He was able to get exactly the same product Salvadore gave me. Hard to believe that it is an over-the-counter medication, considering the amount of codeine it contains!

We turn onto a wider road, not a highway but just wide enough for me not to squirm every time we pass cyclists on their early-autumn Saturday-afternoon outings. Except those who are clearly training for some cycling event, these cyclists are on simple bikes—three speeds, five speeds, even the really old-fashioned "no speed" bikes. In the warm afternoon sun, they seem relaxed, drinking in the fresh air and enjoying one another's company.

Gordon has navigated well. We come to a bustling town. The shop he is looking for is on the main street—a continuation of the country road—so it isn't long before he sees the sign he is seeking: "Nike." That's not the name of the shop, but he's been told that it is the only shop with the word "Nike" in the window.

His purchase doesn't take long. Sure enough, Laura's cousin, the owner of the shop, was expecting him. He has chosen zippered, soft-sided cloth bags—each with a big Nike logo. Wow! We rarely buy name-brand items. I wonder how much they cost. I'm not asking. It's great that he realized we needed them before he started to pack.

After stuffing the bags in the back seat, Gordon heads across the street to the gelato vendor. My, oh my, he and Laura really did have this all planned out! He returns with two cups of gelato. A baby-size one for me, filled with that delicious, rich, sweet, tart citrus explosion—*gelato al limone*. A king-size serving for him with two flavours: dark, bitter chocolate on the bottom, and pale, sweet hazelnut on the top. Yum! With the windows down, we sit in the car, basking in the fact that we are together in a tiny Tuscan town, enjoying the same treat as many others we see meandering along the sidewalk.

Gordon asks how I'm doing before he starts the car to head back to Santa Maria.

In my usual annoying way, I answer with a question: "Why?"

His lips thin into a straight line. I know he really hates it when I do that.

He takes a breath, and then says, "I was thinking we could go to a little delicatessen in Montaione that I've found and we could buy enough food for tomorrow's dinner. It's Sunday tomorrow and I don't know if it will be open. And since we leave early on Monday, it would be nice not to have to prepare food as well as do all the packing up and cleaning. But if you're getting tired, or if the muscle spasms are starting up, we'll go straight home."

"I seem to be okay, so let's go. I'm absorbing as much of this day as I possibly can. I'll be tired by the time we get back, but I need to push myself a bit. As you said, this is a trial run."

We go back the same way we came for a bit, and then we see the directional sign to Montaione. It isn't as far out of the way as we might have thought. We soon recognize where we are and Gordon drives directly to the deli, even though it is a hilltop town and the streets zigzag back and forth, creating terraces of homes, shops, and hotels. The owner is at the door, putting out the "*Chiuso*" sign. We've made it just in time. Gordon is ushered in. They must be having a good time—I can hear lots of laughter. Gordon has the best laugh in the world—it comes from his belly and his heart. It is infectious.

"You're going to love your dinner tomorrow night," he gloats when he returns. "They had grilled zucchini, grilled eggplant, and grilled peppers. It looks like the skins of the eggplant and peppers will come off easily. I wanted to buy some roasted chicken, but they were sold out. I hope ham will be okay?"

What did I do to deserve this kind, gentle, generous man?

I nod my thanks, my eyes on his. Words are not possible.

As we drive home, the sun is low, casting golden radiance on the hills. Windows catch the light, becoming brilliant pieces of gold, amber, and topaz, the countryside an iridescent jewel box filled with treasure.

Gordon doesn't even ask if I will walk from the parking area. He parks as close as he can to the suite, comes around, and gently lifts me out. We walk slowly along the path and up the stairs, arms around each other's waists—for support, and for love.

The chair with its cushions is waiting for me on the porch. It is a welcoming sight. On the table is a fresh vase of roses from the garden. A gift from Clara's family.

Gordon is in the kitchen, putting away his deli purchases, and then he rushes out.

"I forgot. We're supposed to have a FaceTime with Susan. Are you up for it?"

I'm not sure. I look like a corpse. My voice is barely a croak. I'll probably cry. I'm worried I'll scare Ella and Finn.

They're four and two, and they have only ever seen me looking healthy.

Never a poker player, I know the doubt must have paraded across my face.

"I'll be beside you. If you need me to take over, all you have to do is turn the iPad a bit so that you are out of the picture. Susan needs to see you, to reassure herself that you are actually out of the hospital and well enough to come home."

As if to make the point, the iPad in his hand rings. To give me a moment to compose myself, Gordon sets the camera on himself when he answers. Susan and he chit-chat for a moment or two, and then he asks, "I'm sure you'd like to see her for yourself?" Not waiting for the answer, he turns the iPad toward me.

And there is my beautiful daughter, with Ella and Finn both on her lap. We're all silent for a moment, just looking at each other. Finn tries to crawl through the iPad to get to me. I feel just the way he does—so wanting their physical touch. I try to speak, but the emotion of the moment has cancelled the little voice I have. Gordon hadn't told them about the injury to my throat, so they are completely unprepared for my voice. They have a good visit with Gordon. I'm able to stay within view, and that seems to be enough for them.

Gordon prepares the last of the pasta stars for my supper, drizzled with oil and topped with lots of grated Parmesan. I choke down the baby-food vegetables before I allow myself even a taste of the pasta. With the dietary restrictions, and not having our home kitchen, it is tough to get the right balance of foods into me.

Right after supper, I ask Gordon to help me get ready for bed. The day has taken its toll. There won't be any problem with me sleeping tonight. Probably Gordon will appreciate some time to himself. I know he plans to send an email to

Michelle. Like Susan, she has been so good at staying in touch with him, and so supportive.

Before we say good night, I ask to have a banana, a few biscuits, and a jar of applesauce on the bedside table. When I woke up in the middle of last night I was hungry and had to disturb Gordon. Tonight, I want him to sleep through.

15

OCTOBER 7

———

THE FIRST time I wake is when the rooster crows. I surface just enough to enjoy the stirring of the morning from the neighbouring farm and all the surrounding trees. The sounds and songs drift in and around me, a reassuring ritual from time immemorial.

From the bed across the room come snores of a deep, relaxed sleep. Making no noise, I help myself to the breakfast beside me. Gordon wakes up several hours later. I'm smug. The food is gone. He looks rested.

As with every other night since the surgery, I've spent the entire time lying flat on my back. I'm stiff and really need to move, but yesterday's experience has taught us that I need to take the muscle spasm medication before I sit up. Gordon prepares it, bringing a straw with the glass. While he holds the glass for me and I sip, we talk about what we need to do today.

Gordon needs to pack and clean the suite. I need to walk as much as I can—on my own. Gordon suggests that I might

like to take pictures of the roses in the garden. Ever the per-
suasive salesman, he knows my preferences.

It is Clara's christening day. Fortunately for her family,
most of the guests left yesterday, so cleaning for the next
round of guests is all done. It is very quiet. We might even be
the only ones here. It is so peaceful.

Gordon anxiously waits below me as I descend the two
stone steps to the garden pathway. I make it down all by myself! After a few shaky steps forward, I tell him to go and do
his work. I want to enjoy the roses.

There was heavy dew last night. Dewdrops are still
cupped in the velvety petals; the slight breeze in the air
makes the flowers shimmer with ripples of light. Being
alone in a garden is Nirvana to me—breathing in the musky
air of well-tended soil, layered with the rich fragrances of
roses, is restorative beyond compare. By the time I return to
the steps and call out for Gordon to guide me upwards, I've
taken more than physical steps toward recovery. My mind-
set has shifted—just a little—and I'm more confident, more
settled in myself.

My porch chair has been moved—to the bedroom. I'm
to sit in it and direct the packing—well, at least the packing
of my stuff. When I get to the bedroom, Gordon's stuff is
already packed. Even so, the task is pretty complicated. In
the move from the upstairs apartment to this one, things got
muddled. In the end, I suggest that the stuff I need in transit
get packed into one carry-on bag and the rest be packed how-
ever it fits. When we get home, we can sort it out.

As he is packing, I ask, "Where is my jewellery?"

"What jewellery?"

"My wedding and engagement rings. My watch. My sap-
phire earrings."

"Where were they?"

"On the bedside table in the other apartment. I couldn't bear having them on the day I was in so much pain."

"Hmm. I'm not sure."

"Do you remember where you put my travel clock? Maybe you put the jewellery in the same place."

"Yes. I put it in with your lingerie. Oh! Whew! Yes! It's all here."

He brings the jewellery to me. I slip on the rings. They fall off. The watch feels heavy. The holes in my ears have sealed over, and I can't poke the studs through. All of it feels foreign, like someone else's, not mine. He quickly puts the jewellery into a plastic zip-lock bag, and then into my purse, hiding these reminders of how ravaged my body is.

The hard part about packing is figuring out what I will need on our trip home. We're flying from Florence to Frankfurt and staying overnight at the airport hotel. It's just so hard to anticipate how many ostomy bags I'll need, how many bandages, how many drugs and backup clothes. We review what I've used in the past seventy-two hours and decide to pack that much. Since I have to use scissors to prepare the sealer ring for the ostomy and we can't pack scissors in a carry-on, I'll put a fresh one on tomorrow morning, and that will have to do until we get home. Actually, I'm not due to change it until we get home, but I just want to make sure that it is stuck on properly. I don't want any leakages on the trip. How embarrassing would that be?

We check and then double-check. In the end, both packing and cleaning are finished far ahead of anticipated time. It's still early afternoon.

I give Gordon a grin and say, "I bet if I walked by myself to the car, you would be willing to drive into Montaione for one last gelato. I need to see if theirs is better than the ones we had yesterday."

It's a great idea. The day is warm; if we had a convertible, the top would be down. All the windows are rolled down and the fall air caresses our faces as we meander along the narrow roads. The Sunday cyclists are everywhere. We pass by them slowly and receive many appreciative waves. We're in slow mode, relishing our last day in Tuscany. And indeed, the Montaione gelato is better than yesterday's—perhaps because we know it is our last one on this trip. We take detours as we travel back to Santa Maria, extending this Sunday afternoon drive.

When we arrive, we're relaxed and ready to travel tomorrow. I even walk back from the parking area and up the stone steps without help, though I still haven't mastered getting out of the car by myself.

As the sun is setting, we sit on the patio. Gordon has the last of the single malt Scotch he purchased so long ago in the Vancouver duty-free shop. I have a cup of my favourite Italian tea. We talk about what has happened over the past two and a half weeks and how strange it is that we both have truly wonderful memories about the experience—more than anything else, the warmth of the people we have met. We laugh when we think about what I wanted from our Tuscan holiday—to feel we had become a part of life here. We sure did that—but we never expected to become so familiar with the health care system!

No cooking for Gordon tonight. He unwraps deli packages and arranges the selection on the plates. It looks and tastes wonderful.

Our conversation turns to what we can expect at home. My brother Lyle has confirmed that he'll be waiting for us at the airport. Taking public transit, as we had originally planned, is out of the question on this return trip. He's promised to bring some basic groceries for us, too, so that we won't need to shop right away.

And I'm pretty sure our friend Colleen has put some suppers in the freezer for us. She promised to be waiting for us when we arrive home, to help me with whatever I need. Her experience as a palliative care nurse will be helpful; she's gentle and she's had to deal with all the sad facts of deteriorating bodies. I'll be in good hands when I get home.

We are so grateful for all this help.

It's fully dark by the time I'm ready for bed. Once I'm tucked in, we hold on to one another for a few moments—an awkward kind of hug, but oh so lovely. No words are expressed. None are needed. We are going home—together.

16

OCTOBER 8

———

Is it my imagination, or is the rooster particularly proud this morning? He should be proud; he has awakened us both before our alarm rings. We relax and enjoy the morning sounds before stirring. Medication first, then a shower for me, along with changing the ostomy ring.

"Please, God, let it all go well. Let me feel comfortable that everything is secure before we start our travels," I think.

Before we know it, we're waving goodbye to Laura and heading to Florence. Gordon spent quite a while with her trying to get directions to the car rental lot near the Florence airport. We follow Laura's advice and drive to the airport and hire a taxi to show us the way and then take us back to the airport after we drop the car off. With that worry out of the way, we can simply enjoy the trip along the highway to Florence. We're both surprised by how short a distance it is—less than two hours. It took much longer when we arrived. We must have taken a more circuitous route.

The taxi driver is tickled. He'll be getting a substantial fare from us. That's okay. *We're* tickled. We *never* would have found the rental place without him.

Gordon wants me in the taxi while he's in the rental office doing paperwork. But it is a beautiful day and I want to soak up the sunshine, so I decide to practise walking. The road is uneven, so I have to be careful. It takes him too long. I can barely stand up. The taxi driver notices that I'm starting to stumble. He hurries over and gives me support. When we get to the taxi, he soon realizes that I am not able to get in by myself. Just like Gordon, he picks me up and carefully deposits me in the front passenger seat. Once again, I am stunned by the kindness extended to me in this country.

Oh, boy—Gordon is coming out of the office not looking very happy. Surely the company didn't renege on their price quote for the extra time?

He's looking around desperately. The taxi driver calls to him and points at the front seat to show him I am sitting in the car. Relieved, he gets in the back seat.

"What happened? You didn't look very happy when you came out. Did they charge you too much?"

"No—they honoured the agreement we had. But their Visa machine is down, so I couldn't get a receipt. You know that I don't trust car rental companies, so I feel uncomfortable. But they assured me that everything would be all right, and we can't do anything about it anyway, so I'll try to let it go."

Wow—this is a new man in my life. I like it.

If the taxi driver could have parked on the sidewalk to get me closer to the airport entrance, he would have. What an expert! He insists on taking all of our bags to the check-in counter so that Gordon's full attention can be on getting me inside safely. The area is cavernous, without any seats anywhere. When we meet up with the driver, he gestures to the luggage scale, helps me sit down, and then takes my hand, looks into my eyes, and wishes me well.

Finally, we're checked in and it's good news all around. We don't have to pick up our checked baggage in Frankfurt; it's been tagged through to Vancouver. And an attendant with a wheelchair has been assigned to me, which means we're given priority status through security and taken directly to the waiting area. The attendant leaves with assurances she'll be back in time to get us on the plane.

It's well past lunchtime and we're both starving. Gordon goes off to find some food for us, and I "guard" our carry-on bags. We have a chuckle about that. If anyone wanted to take anything, they could. I can't even scream.

"Uh-oh. I have to pee."

Gordon isn't back yet, so I ask an honest-looking person (also the nearest) to look after our bags. And then—"Hmm, I've never driven a wheelchair before. Good—the brake isn't on. I just have to back up a little and then manoeuvre through all these hundreds of moving people over to the restroom. It has a handicapped sign, so I should be okay.

"Man, this is hard work. My arms and shoulders hurt. Damn, I got my finger caught in the wheel again. That hurts!

"Okay. How do I get the door open? There must be an automatic door opener somewhere. I don't see it. I'll just wait until someone comes out."

That doesn't work. By the time the mom with two daughters gets through, the door is closing.

"I really have to pee. What the heck—I'm going to ask that man to open it for me."

He looks a little nervous opening a ladies restroom door, but he does it. I give him the biggest smile of thanks I can muster.

"Whew—the handicapped stall is vacant. Why won't the door open? It isn't locked. What am I doing wrong? Maybe it opens outward? Yes, it does, but how do I pull it open when the wheelchair is blocking the path?"

A young woman comes to my rescue. She holds the door while I wheel through, and then closes it so that I can lock it. I panic.

"What if I fall while I'm in here and the door is locked?" I decide to leave it unlocked. "If anyone sees me, so what?"

The need to pee is really urgent now. I wheel around and face the toilet, and then realize I have to get out of the wheelchair and onto the toilet. My panic about falling is well founded. These are motions I haven't ever done in my life.

"I need to use the wheelchair as a brace. It mustn't move. Where is the brake?"

I fish around and desperately push on a lever near my right hand. I'm in luck. It's the brake.

I squirm forward, inch by inch, keeping my bum solidly on the seat. When I'm right at the edge of the seat, I get both feet on the ground and push myself up using my hands on the arms. This amount of exertion makes me dizzy, so I wait until that passes before I do a turnaround shuffle.

"Now I have to figure out how to lower myself onto the toilet—but first, my panties. Fortunately, I decided to travel in a skirt. Maybe I should have worn a diaper.

"I did it! And I got there in time! Whew! I need to wash more than my hands. Thank you, bathroom designers, for putting a sink in the handicapped cubicle."

You would think that the reverse process would be a whole lot easier, but it isn't. I know what to do, but I'm exhausted. And when I push open the cubicle door, it whacks a little old woman walking past. Thank heavens she seems to be okay.

Gordon is waiting for me. The only thing in the food fair that he thought I could eat was lasagna. To his surprise, I devour the whole thing. He was hoping he would get a bite, to top up his rather small, unappetizing sandwich.

As we are eating, passengers start loading onto buses to take them to our plane, waiting out on the tarmac. We're surprised that we aren't taken first. The departure lounge is almost empty by the time the attendant returns. She's relaxed and smiling, so we relax, too. She takes us out and loads us into something that is like a cherry picker! Only our "bucket" is roomy enough for several wheelchairs and is enclosed with glass. We zoom out to the plane and are raised up to the rear entrance, where there are no stairs, only an open door. The attendant wheels me into the plane. When I feel stable, I stand and clumsily walk up the aisle to our seats.

This leg of the journey is short. There are no business-class seats, but Lufthansa's seating is roomy enough to be tolerable, especially after takeoff, when the seat can recline a bit. We're in the front row. Although I'm short and really don't need the legroom, the visual space helps keep claustrophobia at bay. I rarely experience claustrophobia, but I started to panic as I became enclosed in the plane—perhaps an aftermath of being confined in the hospital, or a fear of something going wrong with my body again.

For most of the flight, we are lost in our own thoughts. Gordon is so worried about me and how I'll be able to handle the journey. I can tell from his shoulders—they're rigid, the way he holds them when he's carrying a lot of stress. Knowing him, he's reviewing every detail again, and again, to make sure he's forgotten nothing. Usually, I try to soothe his worries, but this time I have nothing to offer. I *am* his worry.

The two hours pass quickly. Before we know it, we're in Frankfurt.

Once the plane is empty, an attendant arrives with a wheelchair. I only have to take two steps before I am safely tucked in and whisked away—to a special services counter. They confirm that we are staying in the airport hotel and that our checked luggage will be on our plane tomorrow. We ask them what will be on the menu. They can only reply in general terms, but they ask if we have special dietary needs. When Gordon explains my limited diet, they are very concerned. We should have ordered a special meal, but that must be done more than twenty-four hours in advance. We decide not to worry about it. We can't imagine that at least one of the menus won't work.

Once the folks at the special services counter are satisfied they have done all they can for us, we ask for directions to the hotel.

The attendant comes forward and says, "It is my pleasure to show you the way."

She sure knows how to negotiate her way through this immense, crowded terminal! She pushes the wheelchair and carries one of our bags, while Gordon follows in her wake. As we go, she points out landmarks—we assume so that we won't get lost on our return tomorrow morning.

Within five minutes, we are at the hotel's reception desk. We are already checked in, courtesy of the airline's special services. The attendant passes me and the wheelchair to a hotel employee, who immediately takes us to our room. Gordon hadn't asked for a wheelchair-accessible room, but we've been assigned one. There is space to move around without bumping into furniture, and the bathroom is perfect—grab rails by the toilet, a bulkhead-style shower replete with a bench and shower heads at all angles.

I prefer not to use the wheelchair in the room. The hotel employee is happy to take it away, but insists that he will be back tomorrow morning in time to take us to our flight.

"We have a good relationship with Lufthansa. It is our

pleasure to provide you with this service. What time would you like to wake? I will arrange a call for you."

We agree on a time, he bows, and then he leaves.

Although the shower looks mighty inviting, the bed is calling me. I ask Gordon if he would mind getting me settled and then find something to do so that I can rest. I couldn't have asked for anything better. He's itching to get out and explore the airport—it pulses with activity.

Within moments, I am sound asleep and only stir when Gordon comes back and gently rouses me. It was early afternoon when he left. It's now starting to get dark.

"You need to wake up. If you don't, you may not be able to sleep through the night."

I'm groggy, but I agree.

He looks very pleased with himself. It took him the whole time to explore just the immediate area—grocery stores, fashion shops, bookstores, restaurants, and, yes, I sniff a pub. He had a lovely time having a pint at the bar and people-watching. It is so good to see him looking more relaxed.

As we realize we're hungry, we also realize our mistake. Without the wheelchair, there's no way I can get to a restaurant, even though there is quite a selection right below us in the terminal. Then we see the room service menu. Perfect—a kid's-size portion of spaghetti for me "with lots of grated Parmesan," a clubhouse sandwich for Gordon.

We haven't watched TV for weeks. The time passes as we catch up on world news. I am shocked to learn that my Roma companions were not exaggerating during their late-night whispers—there is a very brief report about protests against the Roma people, so brief I don't register in which country.

The knock at the door comes just forty-five minutes after ordering. We lift the lids from our plates to reveal two enormous servings. The spaghetti would be enough to feed both of us! How much do children in Germany eat? By the time I've had my fill, the serving still looks untouched. Gordon manages to put away all of his clubhouse, the salad, and fries that came with it, though! Comfort foods.

We find a movie and settle in for some entertainment—mainly to stay awake for a little bit. Our flight isn't until mid-morning. I decide to shower when we wake so that I'll be as fresh as possible.

17

OCTOBER 9

———

OUR WAKE-UP call comes as planned. I get into the bathroom, all set for a wonderful shower, washing my hair and everything, but I'm overwhelmed with fatigue. My hair will have to wait. Gordon moves the shower bench close to the sink and I settle for a sponge bath. I am so glad that I changed the ostomy ring yesterday—I couldn't have coped with it today. I even need help getting the bag re-attached; my hands tremor and my fingers are like rubber.

When I'm finally dressed and ready for the trip, breakfast arrives. Although I know I should eat, all I want is a cup of tea and a piece of dry toast. I just can't stomach any more applesauce or another banana.

Worry settles back onto Gordon, but we both know we have no choice but to move forward. Tomorrow, our travel health insurance expires.

It's ten minutes before we're supposed to go and time to give myself the anticoagulant injection. The prepackaged sterile injection, the antiseptic, the sterile cotton swabs, and the instructions in five languages are waiting for me in the bathroom. Dr. Lollio showed me how to pinch the skin and fat on my thigh, and the angle of the needle for the injection. Now all I have to do . . . is do it.

Prepping the skin is fine. Prepping the needle to release any air is fine. Pinching the skin is fine. But jabbing the needle in takes courage, and I have to work very hard to muster enough. My admiration has just deepened for all the people in the world with diabetes, or any other disease, which necessitates doing this daily. Equally, my disbelief has deepened that people actually choose to inject themselves with recreational drugs.

A knock at the door announces the arrival of the wheelchair and the first step of our journey today. Our bill is settled at the front desk in less than a minute, and then we are escorted back to Lufthansa's special services desk and yet another attendant immediately takes us to the departures level and security.

There is a security station set up to screen travellers with unique needs. There's only one person ahead of me, but it seems to take forever before it's finally my turn. The attendant wheels me into the narrow aisle formed by waist-high metal counters. The officer is severe-looking, without a glimmer of human kindness.

She passes the security wand over me. It screams its warning as it passes over my metal stitches. She grunts, puts her wand down, reaches over, digs in, and grabs the whole area with her strong hand, squeezing hard. The pain is shocking. I try to explain the metal stitches.

"*Shweigen!*" she yells. Her meaning is clear: "Silence!"

She feels a lump beside her hand. She grabs the lump, twisting it. With her hand still gripping me, I manage to pull up my clothes so that she can see what is there. The incision is covered with my support belt and the bandage. I offer to remove them both. She smacks my hand away. Then she sees the bag half-filled with shit and realizes what she is holding. She curses, revolted, making a gagging sound. Disgust is written all over her face as she arrogantly throws my passport into my lap and tells the attendant to push me through, my midriff still exposed for everyone to see.

I have shrivelled to a snivelling lump of nothing. A nothing filled with pain and rage. Pain in my tender abdomen, which is worrisome because there had not been pain there previously. Pain of deep humiliation from her disgust at my condition—a humiliation that so many live with every day. And worst of all, a rage of prejudice. That security officer had become everything I loathe and fear—I flash back to my hospital Nazi hallucination—and for a moment, I am blinded by that prejudice, of which I am quickly and deeply ashamed. I struggle to remind myself she was doing her job—a job where soft-heartedness could result in disaster.

As soon we are out of the narrow aisle, my attendant comes around in front of me, shielding me from curious eyes. She leans down and wraps her arms around me, tears sliding down her cheeks.

"I am so sorry. She had no right to hurt you."

Once my clothes are in place again, we move out of the flow of people, waiting for Gordon to clear security. He hurries over. Seeing my face, he asks what happened. It takes a lot of self-control for him not to go back to security and accost the officer. Fortunately, he knows which battles to choose.

We're taken to the executive lounge, where the attendant tells us she will leave us until it is time to board the plane.

"In the meantime," she says, "I'm going to report the behaviour of that security officer to my boss. I don't know if anything can be done, but someone needs to know about it."

None of the chairs looks comfortable—too low, too high, too soft. I feel like Baby Bear in the Goldilocks fairy tale. Gordon finds the buffet and returns with a plate of soft foods.

"You have to eat," he urges. "You've had virtually nothing since supper last night."

I promise to eat something, but I don't promise to eat a lot. Then I tell him to go and explore the duty-free. I know he's anxious to buy something special.

As soon as I'm left alone, the shakes that I've kept under control grip my whole body. It's like I'm in shock. Probably because I *am* in shock. I've survived this whole health crisis by existing in liminal space, just slightly removed from myself and others, removed from most of what was going on. The people around me have cared for me, surrounding me with warmth, concern, protection.

The incident at security clearance stripped all of that away. I'm as raw as a newborn babe just forced from the womb into the harsh light of this world.

Unlike the babe, I *can* return to that liminal space. I'm not ready for ugly reality. If I could, I would curl up into the fetal position in this wheelchair. Instead, I strap myself into the chair, close my eyes, and shut out the world for a while.

The meditation that I need won't come.

What does come is visualization of that perfect light— warm, loving, shimmering. I feel it permeating every part of me—my body, my mind, my soul. And every part of me is soothed by its presence.

When I open my eyes, I'm ready for the journey ahead. But first, I need to tend to myself.

The way to the handicapped washroom is clearly marked. There's a button to open the door. The washroom is huge— plenty of space for a wheelchair, a low table for bags, a sink, a big kind of hair dryer, and near the toilet, a handheld shower and a faucet at waist height.

This looks promising.

There's a good chance that I'll have to change the ostomy bag. When I've scooted my bum forward on the wheelchair,

I manage to place my purse on the seat behind me. I've got two spare bags in there and need to be able to reach them from the toilet.

Sure enough, I discover that the officer dislodged the bag and its contents are oozing out.

"God, it stinks. Okay, I need to do a full cleanup. I can use toilet paper. The faucet is right there, so I can wet the toilet paper while I'm sitting here. I'll need to change my panties—they're a mess. Good thing I put an extra couple of pairs in my purse. I can throw the dirty ones away. I've got it all planned out."

I turn the faucet on just a bit. No water comes out. I turn it on a bit more. I'm drenched! The water came out of the shower head! I have to keep going. I have no choice.

Using the water that landed on the wheelchair seat, I dampen the toilet paper and get the ostomy area cleaned up. Remembering to cover the ostomy hole with more toilet paper, I open my now sopping-wet purse to get a fresh bag and a dry pair of panties.

Attaching the bag and removing my panties is a piece of cake. But how will I get the clean panties on? I can't bend. For that matter, how am I going to pick up the dirty ones that I dropped on the floor?

Holding the panties with one hand, I manage to snag one foot through the proper leg hole. I pull them up a bit, then basically use that leg hole as an anchor and get my other foot through. Since my feet are wet, the panties are now wet—but they're clean.

I decide to use the same technique with the dirty ones, get them on just enough so that I can grab them and then take them off, but hold on to them so that they don't fall onto the floor. It works!

Fortunately, there is a full roll of toilet paper. I have to use a lot of it to dry off the wheelchair before I can climb aboard.

Then, to my amazement and delight, I discover that the big hair dryer is actually a body dryer.

"That makes sense, really. Who travels with a towel? Yet there is a shower in here."

I'm able to dry my hair, panties, skirt, blouse, and even my purse. They may still be damp, but they're no longer dripping wet.

There's a knock at the door. I hear the attendant's voice.

"Are you there? We've been waiting for you for quite a while. It's past time for me to take you to the gate."

I had hoped to take a moment to collect myself, but there isn't time.

Gordon has to hustle to keep up with the attendant. She wheels me right onto the plane and fastens me into my seat, and as soon as she leaves, the doors close and the plane starts to move away from the gate.

We check out our surroundings. Perfect. We're in the first row of business class. The seats are in pairs. I'm on the aisle. The bathroom is ahead of us on the left, just a few steps away. We have no one in front of us. This is home for the next ten hours.

As we're taxiing along the runway, Gordon wants to know if I'm okay. With the engines and the announcements, it's too noisy. I motion that we'll talk later. Hopefully, I can avoid that conversation entirely. My sense of calm has been eroded. I really need it back, and talking about how I'm doing isn't going to help.

Once we're in the air, he doesn't press his question. Instead, he finds my earbuds, plugs them in, and lets me find classical music. The familiar sound of Pachelbel's Canon in D is a welcome retreat. I find myself relaxing into the repetitive, stately harmony of cello and violin.

Apparently, I have been sleeping soundly. The first round of drinks has already been served and it is time to order dinner. Neither of the choices are possible options for me—a German sausage plate or a spicy chickpea curry. The flight attendant isn't sure there is anything on the plane that will be suitable, but she promises to check out the other menus. Gordon happily orders the chickpea curry.

She comes back carrying a plate of food. She's served it from the captain's own food locker—smoked salmon, crackers, grapes, and some pâté. Gordon reaches into his bag and pulls out some Babybel cheeses that he bought last night at a grocery store in the terminal.

Memory of Dr. Bing's question "Did you have any fish?" makes it hard for me to dig into the smoked salmon, but after the first bite I remember how much I enjoy it. I examine every morsel for the tiniest of bones, and I do find one but am enjoying the flavour so much, I choose not to worry that I'll actually swallow one. And although grapes aren't on my recovery food list, mainly because they have skins, I decide to take the risk, chewing them so thoroughly no pieces of skin are left.

The flight attendant comes along for a chat while we eat. She is curious about what happened to me on our trip. By the time Gordon finishes the story, she is struggling to contain her tears.

We can tell she is genuine when she says, "Please tell me if there is anything we can do to make you more comfortable."

She leaves, then returns right away.

"In about half an hour there will be a lineup for the toilet, and then again after the movie is finished. You might want to use it now, so you don't have to wait. And also, because there are no seats in front of you, often people think they can stand there. You can prevent that by putting some bags on the floor."

I take her advice, and am I ever glad. Although I changed the ostomy bag at the airport, stuff is still oozing out. On closer examination, I discover that the security officer broke the seal between the beeswax ring and my skin. There is nothing I can do. I don't have a spare ring with me. After cleaning it as best I can, I pack a wad of toilet paper on top of the ring. I'll be making many visits to the toilet, I guess. I would hate to be the cause of a serious stench on board. Thank heavens I haven't eaten much in the past twenty-four hours.

I return to my seat and ask Gordon to help me get settled for a long sleep—extra pillows, two blankets, my eye mask, and earbuds in case I want more music.

Before he hands me the earbuds, though, he says, "What's wrong? Something happened in the toilet. I can tell."

I tell him the seal is broken and then ask him, "If you start to smell me, please wake me up so that I can get cleaned up again."

He knows how fastidious I am, how much I hate this bag, and how embarrassed I would be to be smelly.

His face fills with sympathy and love. As he is wont to do, he gently touches me on the top of my head.

"Of course," he replies.

I sleep well. There is yogourt, cookies, and tea for breakfast. I can't stomach porridge, and eggs are off limits. Lesson learned. If travelling when ill, order a special menu. All that is soon forgotten, though. Vancouver is in sight and in beautiful sunshine. We're almost home.

We taxi to the gate. The rest of the passengers exit the plane. The Lufthansa staff come to say goodbye to us. And then we wait for Lufthansa's partner airline, Air Canada, to provide a wheelchair. Eventually, someone comes to tell us that all the wheelchairs are taken and I will have to walk off the plane and up the ramp to the airport, where we will be picked up in one of the airport carts. No amount of protesting works. We have to leave the plane. I have to walk into the terminal.

I wore compression stockings for the flight and exercised my legs as much as possible, but my feet and legs have still become very swollen. It is agony to put weight on them. The ramp is uphill, making it even more agonizing. By the time I get to the terminal, I am drenched in sweat, almost delirious with exhaustion. The transportation isn't waiting for us, nor is anyone here to help us. Gordon gets me into a chair and goes to look for help. The look on his face tells me he's more likely looking to make trouble—for someone, anyone!

He comes back with an Air Canada representative and won't let him leave our sides. The transport cart finally arrives, but there are no lower seats and no one is willing to move. I have to climb up the ridiculous, slippery, steep steps to an equally ridiculous, tiny seat, bumping my incision on the sharply turned handrails and my shins on the steps on my ascent. I nearly pass out. In the meantime, Gordon is straddling the cart and the floor, refusing to budge until the representative agrees to come with us to make sure a wheelchair is available for me to get to the car. Tempers are flying all around us—passengers, cart driver, Air Canada representative. But Gordon does not give up. Eventually, he gets his way; a wheelchair is waiting where we need it.

Waiting anxiously at the door of the arrivals area is Lyle. The sight of his face triggers a flood of emotions—I don't know what they all are, but for sure one is relief. Relief and familiarity. I have loved my brother all of my life, as he has loved me. I'm just so glad to see him.

He doesn't know it, but I saw that split second of shock on his face. It's the same shock that I saw on my own face when I looked in the mirror that first time in the hospital and saw my mother's face as it was in her last days. It's true—I look like a corpse, my mother's corpse.

He stands beside me, one hand on my shoulder gently massaging, gently reassuring.

Gordon arranges for a porter to help with the luggage, and then my brother leads the way to the car, pushing me in the wheelchair. The representative trails behind, objecting that the wheelchair isn't allowed out of the building. My brother ignores him and continues to the car park. Gordon has to deal with objections, too. The porter refuses to go out of the terminal building without renegotiating the price. As a result, they lose sight of Lyle and me, and it takes them a while to find us.

But we are on our last leg home: from the airport through downtown Vancouver to Horseshoe Bay, where we will take the Bowen ferry, a twenty-minute ferry ride, and finally a ten-minute drive to our home. The traffic is light through Vancouver, and we hit green lights all the way, so we make it from the airport to Horseshoe Bay in record time. Not only that, but we only have fifteen minutes to wait for the ferry. We're all quiet while we wait, lost in our thoughts, wanting to talk but afraid to get started—too much, too serious, too emotional.

We are just glad to be together.

As the ferry comes into Snug Cove and we disembark, instead of being thrilled to be almost home, all I can think is: "How are we going to manage? How is Gordon going to manage—the house; the cleaning; the cooking; the laundry; the shopping; lifting me; walking Gibson, our golden retriever; not to mention getting us to health care appointments that will surely happen sooner than later?" My brooding doesn't take long to morph into full-fledged despondency.

We drive down our steep road and turn into our yard. There, sitting in the sunshine waiting for us, is Colleen. Gordon and Lyle help me out of Lyle's high SUV. I am immediately enfolded in Colleen's arms, my face buried in her raspberry pink cashmere V-neck sweater.

"Oh, you poor, poor dear. You look so sick. I can't believe they allowed you to travel this way. I'm here to help—whatever you need, I'll do it."

Her warmth, her character, her friendship are exactly what I need. To her, I can admit that I am filthy and too tired to do anything about it.

We walk slowly along the covered front porch. We enter the house—it is filled with vases of fresh-cut flowers.

"People heard you were coming home today. They wanted you to know that you are loved. They were left at the door, but I was worried that the deer would eat them, so I brought them inside," Colleen says.

In our bedroom, on the bureau, is another arrangement of flowers.

"These are from Peter and me. We wanted to make this room special for you."

Special, indeed. There is also a comfortable-looking single bed covered with a pretty duvet and plenty of pillows. Our bed is very high, thanks to the deep cushion-topped mattress we purchased last year, so it will be a while before I am able to get into it, even with Gordon's help.

The bathroom is where we are headed, though. And here, ever the nurse, Colleen has magically placed sterile wipes, a gentle cleanser, and a chair. Gordon brings in the bag of backup ostomy supplies.

"So tell me what I need to do," she says.

I've lost all modesty. We just get my clothes off so that Colleen can see for herself.

"I've changed ostomy bags before, of course, when I was nursing in palliative care. But I haven't ever changed a ring before. I'll try my best."

"You'll do better than I possibly could right now," I assure her.

When she pries the ring completely off, she clucks her concern. "This skin looks raw. I hate to put another ring on, but I guess there isn't any choice. I'll clean it with lots of warm sterile water and then let it air-dry a bit."

Just then, some excretion shoots out.

"Oops! I forgot to tell you to cover it with toilet paper."

We both chuckle.

"Did they really think you could look after this yourself?" she asks. "I can't believe you have been able to do it at all. You're just so weak, and this is awkward—especially getting the bag clicked on just right."

With that done, she wants to check the incision. She's concerned about the pain I felt when the security officer in Frankfurt grabbed it. Gently, oh so gently, she removes the bandages. There is blood on them. One of the staples was dislodged and caused the bleeding, but the incision itself seems fine. She massages away the blood with sterile water and then applies a fresh bandage.

Using my own skin cleanser from the counter, Colleen washes my face—and that simple, soothing act eases my worries, even freshens me a bit. Noticing that I've begun to shiver, she goes to the closet and returns with my favourite pink terrycloth bathrobe. It is exactly what I need right now.

"Thank you."

Our eyes lock, and I know that she has understood the depth of my thanks.

We make our way to the living room, where a quandary awaits. Do we have a chair that I can sit in?

Colleen sees that Gordon and I need to sort things out for ourselves.

On her way out the door, she says, "I'll come any time you need me. Just call. Oh—and there's dinner in the fridge for you."

When the door closes, Gordon and I stand for a minute, looking at each other, feeling such gratitude for everything.

Then Gordon says, "I could use a hug."

It feels so good to be in each other's arms, being one, together—standing in the middle of our living room, surrounded by the life we have built together.

The wooden rocking chair turns out to be a perfect place for me to sit. It is upright, sturdy, the right height, has arms for leverage, and the rocking motion assists in getting in and out. Once cushions are adjusted and a cup of tea is within reach on a side table, Gordon sits beside me.

"We have something to talk about," he begins. "On the plane, a B.C. physician was sitting across the aisle from me. He noticed how weak you were. I explained what had happened and expressed my concern that I didn't know the best way for you to get into the B.C. health care system.

"His response was immediate: 'As soon as you can, take her to an emergency department, where there will be access to all forms of screening and to specialists. She may have to wait because she isn't in crisis, but she will get the attention, scrutiny, and care she requires.' I asked him if it mattered which ER you went to and he said to go to the closest one.

"So, I know that you have had a very long day today. And I know it has been exhausting for you. But I would like to take you to the ER tomorrow morning. He says that the best time would probably be around 10:00 a.m., when the night's emergencies have been taken care of and before the late-morning rush. He says that's the usual pattern of ERs. Do you think you could do it?"

"I'll try."

"Good. Let's have Colleen's supper and then get you to bed."

Colleen knows comfort food—macaroni and cheese from Bowen's own Ruddy Potato kitchen. It's rich and creamy, but that's a good thing, since all I can manage are a few bites. Even that small amount provides some calories. It has been a long day with not a lot of food.

18

OCTOBER 10

SLEEP CAME easily last night, but I wake before dawn even without the rooster's announcement. Gordon is still snoring. I hope he didn't hurt his back last night when he moved me into position on this low bed. I need to figure out how to get in and out of bed without risking him being injured.

These thoughts are pushed out of my mind by the alarm clock, which he doesn't hear, and the challenge of how to wake him. I'm next to the window, with the wooden blinds lowered. I rattle them. The alarm plus the wood rattling against the window is loud enough to wake him. He opens his eyes, sees me, and smiles.

"Good morning. Ready for another big day?"

I return his smile and nod. He looks pleased.

He stoops to pick me up. He bends his knees, but even though I've lost at least twenty-five pounds in the past couple of weeks and am now basically skin and bones, I'm still not a lightweight. I can tell the motion required of him is not easy.

But once again, he gets me upright, with wet diaper off, support belt on, and ready to be dressed. We've developed quite a routine, but every day a pant leg or a sleeve gets twisted, and that makes us laugh. What a pair we are!

Our morning plans go without a hitch. We get to the ferry in plenty of time for the sailing we want, and a twenty-minute drive on the other side gets us to the North Vancouver Lion's Gate emergency room at 10:15 a.m.

Although the waiting area is empty, just as we arrive so does an ambulance with someone in great distress. As it should, all attention goes to her, but not long after, I am called to triage for assessment.

Gordon has become skilled at telling my medical history. He is thorough and focussed. He produces his purple file folder with all the information from Italy. They dig right into it. When they see that some of the information is written in Italian, they call for a translator.

"Do you have any allergies?"

"Yes. Quinine and morphine."

"Quinine? How do you know?"

"I was in Africa for two years in the 1960s. Quinine was the prophylactic for malaria back then. It caused intestinal migraines, so I stopped taking it."

"Really? I've never heard of that before. Did you get malaria?"

"Yes."

"And morphine. What does it cause?"

"Horrific hallucinations. It happened in Italy."

"That's not uncommon."

The triage nurse snaps a white hospital bracelet onto my wrist with warnings: "MORPHINE. QUININE." He immediately takes me to the emergency ward, down the corridor and then into a cubicle, where I am once again surrounded by privacy curtains—back in a hospital cocoon.

Usually, waiting is hard for me—I'm not a patient person. If there's something to be done, I like to get it done. And there's always something to be done.

But once again, I'm being taught the discipline of patience. There is nothing for me to do but wait. And the simple act of waiting allows me to re-enter that place of acute awareness, which extends beyond my own body. I am struck by the serenity of the emergency ward—the voices of calm authority subsuming the sounds of those in distress; the unhurried, purposeful footsteps pushing a blood collection cart with its distinctive tinkling sound of test tubes rattling in their metal holders. The serenity touches me to the core—knowing that those who need care the most will receive it, and knowing that this time, I'm the one to wait.

Time passes. I am at peace. Waiting is a blessing.

There is a lull. Patients have been sent to the radiology department for X-rays, for ultrasounds, for CT scans. The blood collection cart has made three return trips. Two patients have been sent for casts—one a leg, another an arm. Several have made their way to the first aid station.

Silence on an emergency ward must be rare. I'm given the privilege of hearing it, appreciating it.

The privacy curtain is opened without a sound.

"Hello, I'm Dr. Chan. I'm the ER physician on duty today. I've read your chart and talked to the triage team, but if you wouldn't mind, I'd like to hear about what happened, directly from you. Then we can decide how to proceed."

I start my story from the point of the pain.

He interrupts and asks, "How long had you been in Italy? Were you anywhere else before that?"

So I start my story again, this time including our days in Paris, in Florence, and our one day exploring Tuscany before the pain. As Dr. Bing did, he asks about what foods I had eaten, whether I had been feeling unwell or dizzy, if I had had any injury.

Satisfied with the information, he asks me to return to "the pain" and subsequently what I remember. Dr. Chan listens, makes notes, and seems to be comparing what I'm saying with whatever information he has in my chart.

I finally stop talking.

He asks, "What happened to your voice?"

I then remember to mention that I'd ripped the nasogastric tube out during one of my hallucinations.

"Was there blood?" he asks.

"Yes, a lot of it," I reply.

He makes another note. Except for the scratching of his pen, there is silence.

He sighs. "I'm sorry about your vacation. I hope you get a chance to return to Tuscany soon. It is one of my favourite places. My wife and I are going there next week for a holiday. It is a delayed honeymoon," he says. "Okay. I agree with the triage team," he continues. "We need to get a full work-up of your blood and an X-ray of your lungs. I'd also like to examine your incision and the ostomy area to make sure everything is healing well.

"Dr. Lewis is the surgeon on call today, so he will be assigned your case. Once I've examined you, I'll speak with him to see if he wants any other tests done. He's in surgery right now, but between patients he always checks in with us. He'll have your chart accessible online. I'll send someone in with a gown."

The "someone" arrives. She has a gown and slipper-socks. She gives me the standard instructions: "All clothes off except your panties, gown on with the opening in the back, then lie down on the bed."

I've been sitting in a chair all this time. I look at the bed. It's too high for me to get onto, and I don't see any hydraulic mechanism to lower it. I explain my predicament. She looks at me as if I'm a full-blown hypochondriac, but she shrugs, bends down at the end of the bed, and uses a crank to lower it—definitely something I could not have done!

With that, she leaves. The curtains aren't silent when "someone" handles them.

It takes me ages to get my clothes off. I'm still struggling with the gown when Dr. Chan returns. With him are two young people in hospital garb. I have no idea what they are doing here, but I ask them to help me with my gown, and then to support me while I attempt to get onto the bed. It has to be lowered some more. Eventually, I can sit on the edge, but one has to swing my feet onto the bed while the other supports my head into position. I apologize for being so weak.

"Well, you've met them now, but I'd like to introduce them. These are our newest residents in the E R—Christopher Alby and Jennifer Carter. They started with us on Monday. I've asked them to join me in examining you. Is that all right with you?"

I nod.

"Good. Let's get started. Oh, you're still wearing a support belt."

"Yes, I was told that I should wear it for at least two months."

"Hmm."

Once my panties are lowered discreetly and the support belt is undone, Dr. Chan inspects the incision and the ostomy area. He sees a small incision on either side, just below my pelvic bone.

"What are these?"

"The surgeons in Italy told me they were going to try laparoscopic surgery, but in the end, they had to do a full incision."

"That makes sense. Your incision has healed nicely. I think it is time to remove the staples, even though one appears to have pulled a bit, causing some bleeding." (I don't bother telling him about the security-officer incident.) "Removing your staples would be good practice for our two residents. Would that be okay with you?"

Dr. Chan is looking directly at me. I have to tell him the truth.

"Although I am always committed to further education and skill development, I'm not sure whether this is my time to be a guinea pig. My body and my mind have been through so much." I turn to the residents. "Have you ever removed staples before?"

They shake their heads. This doesn't help.

Dr. Chan remains silent, just looking at me. He seems to understand my reluctance, but he can see me processing his request. So he is patient, waiting.

"I'll tell you what. If you show them how to remove two staples, I'll rate the pain on a scale of one to ten, with ten being the highest. Then each of them can remove two staples. If I get the same level of pain with them as I do with you, they can continue with the rest. If they cause any pain more than two notches above, I'd like you to finish."

A faint smile shows on his face. I catch him just in time.

"But you have to do *your* best, too."

We all have a chuckle, and the tension is released.

Christopher swabs the incision area. He misses the uppermost part of the incision, which Jennifer quietly points out.

From a sterile tray, Dr. Chan picks up the staple remover. It looks remarkably like the staple remover I have at home, except sturdier. He inserts it and with a gentle tug removes his first staple. It really didn't hurt, but I give his first removal a score of two. His next one is better; it gets a one.

Dr. Chan passes the instrument to Christopher. He's very nervous, taking a lot of time getting the instrument into position. He clearly doesn't know how to use it, so Dr. Chan patiently talks him through the process. Eventually, a staple is removed. It definitely scores a four, but I give it a three to encourage him to do a better job with his second one. He does; this one truly is a three.

Jennifer is next. She has now seen four staples removed, and she seems pretty relaxed. Her first one comes out without any pain. I give her a zero, much to Dr. Chan's surprise. She gets overly confident with her second one, and I flinch a little. That was a four. Maybe she should try a third. She does, and it is a one.

"Okay, they can take the rest out, as long as they don't increase the pain level."

We all agree, but Dr. Chan is called to an urgent case, so it doesn't matter—Christopher and Jennifer will be taking the staples out no matter what pain level they inflict.

They are careful, and very, very slow. Although the pain is minimal, the effort of remaining absolutely still while having two intensely nervous amateurs remove what has held me together for nearly three weeks gets to be too much. I ask them to take a break and just let me breathe for a moment. They are immediately concerned that they've caused too much pain. I don't have the energy to reassure them any more than to shake my head. They offer me a sip of water. That helps, and they return to their task.

Finally, all twenty staples are out. There's a bit of blood, but not as much as I had expected. Christopher disappears to fetch Dr. Chan, while Jennifer swabs the area again, removing the blood. My clotting is good. No fresh blood appears.

Christopher returns to get Jennifer, who quickly covers me with a sheet before she leaves, closing the curtains.

The curtains are still moving when I hear the blood collection cart approaching. This time it comes into my cubicle, along with a cheery person pushing the cart. She announces that she "has come to take my blood." She seems genuinely confused when I ask if she is my vampire. So much for morbid humour. How stupid am I? She's about to stick a needle into my arm.

Dr. Chan must have ordered every blood test available. I lose count after four test tubes are filled.

Thinking it is time to wait some more, I close my eyes and seek the serenity I had found earlier. But waiting isn't for me right now. An orderly comes in and transfers me to another bed.

"We're going to get an X-ray," he says.

I bite my lip and don't verbalize my thought: "Why would *you* want to be in *my* X-ray?"

There's no waiting down in the X-ray department, either. It takes longer to travel back and forth than it does to actually get the X-ray. I wonder why it is possible to have X-rays done by portable machines that come to the patient in Italy but not in Canada? I find the difference to be so interesting. If both methods are equally helpful for diagnosis, imagine the cost savings—less space, fewer orderlies, fewer portable beds, less linen, less cleaning.

Gordon is waiting in the cubicle on my return. In his hand is a takeout bowl. Whatever is inside smells heavenly.

"I checked at the admitting desk. You can have something to eat. I thought that udon would be good—you've been wanting chicken broth for days. This is the closest I could get."

Its tantalizing smell is matched by its taste.

I ask what he's been doing since he left.

"Lots of errands—bank and several grocery stops. And I had lunch at the Japanese restaurant just down the street. It was so good I decided to bring the udon to you. We need to go there together sometime. What's been going on here?"

I fill him in on all the activity. We're both impressed with how quickly I've been looked after, and how thoroughly. We both hope that today is it for hospitals for a while, though in three weeks I should be having the resection surgery to reconnect my bowel.

Dr. Chan surprises us both. He approaches *so quietly.* With him is someone new.

"This is Dr. Richard Lewis. As I mentioned, he will be your surgeon. Is this your husband?"

We do introductions all around. Dr. Lewis tells us that tomorrow Dr. Chan completes his ER residency, and then he's off to Italy to celebrate with his wife of three months.

Dr. Lewis wastes no time. He examines the incision and the ostomy, remarking on how well the incision has healed.

"It is a nice, clean, straight incision. The ostomy looks a little raw. I'll try to get the ostomy care nurse here to take a look. Dr. Chan has looked after you well. He's ordered all the tests you need right now. The results should be ready by tomorrow afternoon. Could you come to my office? I'll let my staff know that you'll be calling for an appointment. The person you'll speak to is Carmen. Here's my card. See you tomorrow."

As he leaves the cubicle, he's texting on his phone.

The two new residents return with sterile gauze and tape to cover the incision. While they're working, a nurse arrives.

"Hi! I'm Elaine from the Ostomy Care Unit. Dr. Lewis asked me to drop in on my way home."

She examines me and says, "Hmm. He wasn't kidding. Your ostomy looks sore. Does it feel sore?"

"I don't have any feeling there. I think the nerves haven't repaired themselves yet."

She nods. "It would be great if you could come in tomorrow morning at around nine thirty. I don't have any clients booked until ten thirty, so I could squeeze you in. I know you live on Bowen, so I apologize for the early start.

"I think your ostomy is healing nicely, but that means that the hole is getting smaller. As a result, your gastric juices are getting onto tender new tissue and causing the inflammation. I'd like to outfit you with a smaller seal unit. In fact, I think we have some choices that would be a lot easier for you to manage. It might take a bit of time, so I'd like a full hour with you. Can you make it here by nine thirty?"

Both Gordon and I nod. How can we say no?

"It's a date, then," she says.

The new residents have stayed for Elaine's examination. After she leaves, we ask if we can go home. They promise to find out. Within moments, they are back to tell us we are free to go, but then Gordon confounds them with a question: "Where do we get a TAP form?"

"What's a TAP form?"

"It's a form that we have to fill in to get our ferry transportation costs covered by the Ministry of Health."

"Maybe you could get one at the ER admitting desk?"

Gordon wraps the support belt onto me and then helps me slide off the bed onto my feet. Once I'm safely in the chair, he gives me my clothes and leaves in pursuit of the pink TAP form. He's got plenty of time; I'm a slow dresser these days.

I'm still struggling to slide my feet into my shoes when he returns holding the form. He kneels and helps me, buckling the shoes as well.

An orderly with a wheelchair arrives. Gordon leaves to get the car so that he can pick me up at the ER entrance.

And just like that—I'm out of the hospital and going home again.

We don't say much until we get to the ferry terminal, but as soon as the car's engine is switched off, we both say at the same time: "That's a relief!"

"You go first—what's a relief?"

He replies, "I was really worried that we would have a lot of bureaucratic glitches. And I was also worried that we might be told that you're healthy enough, you don't need to be using the ER. I'm so relieved that I didn't have to get into any arguments or try to persuade people to do their jobs. They did what I had hoped they would do—looked after you and got the specialists involved right away. What's a relief for you?"

"Well, of course the same as for you. But also—I've met the doctor who will do the resection surgery, and I can hardly wait! Gordon, I was wondering if you would call Sandy for a physiotherapy appointment. We both trust her advice. I'm really worried that you are going to hurt yourself lifting me in and out of bed. I need to learn how to move myself around."

As soon as we're on the ferry, Gordon calls Sandy and leaves a voice mail. No sooner does he finish his message than boarding begins. Our timing is working well today.

The ferry is our island's floating community centre. It's a great place to socialize. It doesn't take much encouragement for him to leave me in the car to find friends on board. He is the gregarious one of the two of us. He needs people. Silence is good for me. The sailing goes quickly for both of us, as does our drive home.

As we are eating supper, the phone rings.

"You would come to our home?" Gordon asks. "Oh, yes, that would be wonderful. Thank you."

He tells me, "That was Sandy. She's coming here when she finishes her last client. She says she'll be here in about an hour. She had heard about your surgery and thought you might need some help right away, before you can make it to her office."

"Gosh! How very thoughtful. How kind."

When Sandy arrives, she apologizes for being a few minutes late. We can't be anything but grateful for her coming at all! It's 7:30 p.m.; she has had a long day. That doesn't stop her from being her usual thorough, professional self.

She wants all of the details of the surgery, of our trip home, and of our concerns right now. As we talk, she makes detailed, handwritten notes. When we finally run out of things to say, she puts her clipboard down on the sofa and asks me to stand up, then sit down, to raise one leg, then the other while seated. She watches as I struggle, then writes more notes. Eventually, she comes over to me and manipulates first my right leg, then my left, watching my face. As she is still holding my left calf, she asks if I have any pain other than what I have already described.

"Yes, as a matter of fact, I do."

"Where?"

"Right where you are holding my leg."

"Describe the pain."

"It's deep. It's constant."

As if my leg is suddenly too hot to handle, she quickly lowers my leg and removes her hand. "Do you notice that your left leg is more swollen than your right leg?"

I nod.

"When did you first notice the pain?"

"I've had it pretty well since the surgery."

"Did you tell anyone about it?"

"No. It seemed the least of my worries. It was bearable."

Sandy looks serious. "When you see Dr. Lewis tomorrow, you need to tell him about the pain. I'm pretty sure he will want you to have an ultrasound of the area."

"Do you think it might be a deep-vein thrombosis or something?"

"I think there is a chance of that, yes. But Dr. Lewis may have a different opinion."

"Well, if it is, how lucky am I that Dr. Lollio provided an anticoagulant injection for the trip home?"

"We're *all* lucky," she replies.

"Now let's go to the bedroom so that I can show you an easy way to get in and out of bed. I'll need a big plastic bag—a garbage bag would be fine."

She shows us something so simple we can't believe everyone doesn't know about this technique. She puts the unfolded bag onto the bed and has me sit on it. Then, using my bum as a pivot point, she lifts my legs and swings them onto the bed while I prop myself up with my arms. Then she helps me lower my back and head down. At no time does she bear my full weight. Getting up is just the reverse! And what she does next is not at all unexpected—she is so methodical, so precise in educating her clients. Gordon and I must repeat the whole sequence, to make sure we know what we're doing. It works! The plastic bag is slippery, allowing my body to move without resistance.

"That's enough for now. Next week will be early enough to start some core-strength exercises. Do you think you'll be able to come to my office?"

"Yes, of course," we reply in unison.

Sandy promises to check her schedule and then call us tomorrow with a time that would work for her. Our goodbyes are filled with profuse thanks. Her response is her typical little shrug and shy smile.

As the door closes behind her, for the first time I feel optimistic about our ability to cope with my physical limitations. I know that she will help us find practical solutions for each and every physical challenge I face.

The ease of getting me into bed is proof of that belief. I no longer need to worry about Gordon's back, and because I am so much more relaxed, I'm pretty sure he is less stressed as well.

"Thank you, Sandy," I whisper before falling asleep.

19

OCTOBER 11

THE ALARM goes off at 6:00 a.m., but Gordon is already out of bed. I can hear him puttering in the kitchen. He must have his hearing aids in, because he comes to shut off the alarm.

"Tea is ready. Let's get you up. Since it is Friday and usually the early ferries are busy, we need to get in the lineup at just after seven thirty if we're going to get to the hospital on time."

Getting up is as easy as going to bed. The plastic bag is a new tool in our arsenal.

Getting going is a different matter. For some reason, I'm all thumbs. Nothing goes together properly—from securing the clean ostomy bag to putting on my clothes, everything gets tangled, doesn't fasten, drops out of my reach. Fortunately, Gordon is ready early and is able to take the time to get me ready, too.

We make it to the ferry lineup later than planned but just in time. We can relax. We're going to be on the eight-thirty ferry, and it is running on time. Everything is fine.

Elaine greets us as soon as we get to the Ostomy Care Unit. She ushers me into the room and asks me to climb up on the bed and loosen my clothes so that she can get to work on my ostomy care.

I look at her in total disbelief. "I can't do that, especially with the bed up as high as it is."

Fortunately, Gordon is still out in the hallway, so he comes in to help. Knowing that he'll have to help me get off the bed and get dressed, he decides to wait rather than to go off for a coffee or an errand. Poor guy, he isn't getting many breaks these days.

Elaine notices the support belt when she comes back in. "Are you still wearing that?"

"Yes, of course. I was told by the staff in Italy that I had to wear it all the time."

"Well, that was probably to help you get around easier in the hospital, but you need to rely on your muscles to hold you upright. You shouldn't be wearing it anymore." She removes the belt from under me and folds it up, signalling that she means business.

She removes the bandage and inspects the whole area. "What are these two small incisions?"

I explain once again about the attempted laparoscopic surgery.

"The incisions are healed. The sutures should come out."

"I would love that—they are driving me nuts."

"There are a couple of sutures that were under the staples. They should come out, too, I think. I'll call Dr. Lewis right now and get his permission."

Sure enough, he responds within minutes to her voice mail message. He apparently asks some questions, because she pokes and prods the areas. As the call ends, she says, "Okay."

She looks at me and says, "You are so lucky to have Dr. Lewis as your surgeon. If I ever had to have any surgery, he would be my first choice."

They are reassuring words, and much appreciated.

She has prepared trays of sterile instruments—all she needs are sterile wipes, surgical scissors, and tweezers. The sutures in the laparoscopic incisions are tight. She has to tug to get them out, but it doesn't hurt. The sutures in the big incision are buried a bit, but even though she has to dig, I don't feel anything. I guess the nerve endings really haven't reconnected yet.

"That's done. Now let's get down to our real business."

She pulls out a chart—pictures of various ostomy products. "This is what you have," she says, pointing to one. "As you know, you have to cut the hole in the seal to size. And it isn't easy to empty the bag and reuse it. Now that you are eating more, you'll find that you will go through a lot of bags. That will be expensive, even though you have extended health benefits."

She points to a different picture as she says, "This style is one of my favourites. My clients find it quite comfortable to wear. It doesn't make you hot as it lies against your belly, and it is easy to empty. You only replace it every three to four days, when it starts to get a bit soggy feeling. You have a flat tummy, so I think it would work well for you. Let's get this old bag and seal off, get you cleaned up, and then measure you."

As she gently removes the seal, she murmurs, "Oh, you poor dear, this does look sore. I was worried it might be when I examined you yesterday. I'll clean the area and then we'll let it air-dry for a bit while we talk about the different products and what you need. I've got samples here, so you can see them all. I can also answer any questions you might have about living with an ileostomy."

My response is silence.

She looks at me. "What are you thinking? Silence usually means avoidance in this unit."

"My mother had a colostomy. She was fastidious. She was glad that it gave her extra years. But watching her live with it, I vowed that I would never opt for that way of life. If I had been told in Italy that it would be permanent, I would have refused surgery. But because they promised it would be temporary, I agreed."

"How do you feel now?"

"It is the most degrading thing I've ever experienced, and I've had some pretty degrading things happen to me."

She sighs. "I know you won't believe me right now, but you honestly can adapt to this even on a permanent basis."

"I don't think so. My husband and I have always enjoyed our sex life. I'm pretty sure I wouldn't be able to overcome this, combined with some history of poor self-image. I definitely don't think I could ever feel sexually attractive with an ostomy. Thankfully, it is temporary. If it isn't, I don't know what I'll do."

She covers the hole with some gauze and then pulls out the options she thinks will work for me. I can see why her favourite would be the most comfortable to wear. Not surprisingly, it is also the most expensive option, but since I'll be having the resection surgery soon, I don't worry.

She takes a gadget that's kind of like a knitting needle-size gauge and puts it over the hole. I'm surprised at how tiny it is. No wonder my skin got raw—the holes I've been cutting in the seals have been much larger; in fact, I'm not sure I could cut the hole that small. It's a good thing Dr. Lewis wanted me to come here right away. I could have caused myself some serious damage.

The seal for this unit is more flexible and thinner than the one I've been wearing. It feels much less obtrusive.

The important thing, I am told, is to have the bag positioned so that it crosses my tummy at an angle. If it hangs vertically, when it gets full, it will pull on the seal and that could cause "problems." I can imagine what kind of problems. I don't need the details.

"Now, the great thing about this product is how easy it is to empty. See the bottom of the bag? It's designed like a dry bag—it folds over itself and then fastens with Velcro. When it's full, while sitting on the toilet, you lean over a bit so that the bag falls between your legs and empty it! Isn't that great?" she says happily.

It's really too bad I can't laugh out loud. The image of me doing all of that without making a disastrous mess cracks me up!

But I nod politely. "Right. That sounds good."

"You don't believe me, do you?"

"Not really."

"Next time you see me, you'll be telling me how well it works, I promise."

"If you say so."

"Okay. You'll need to change the seal once a week. I'm going to give you four seals, but I'd like you to come back in three weeks to get resized."

"In Italy, they told me I should have the resection surgery in six weeks, and that was already almost four weeks ago, so I probably won't need to do that."

"Hmm. Well, just in case, you should make an appointment with me for three weeks from now before you leave, okay?"

"Fine. If you think so."

"I do. Now, here is the order form for the bags and the other supplies I recommend. The supplier ships by courier, so you should get your order within twenty-four hours, but I know that you live on an island, so I'll give you a few bags to carry you through in case delivery takes longer. In addition to a box of bags, you might want to order the deodorant that you can put into the bag and perhaps the room freshener spritzer, as it works very well."

Well, I guess that's it. I'm clean. I have a new "appliance" (the nice word I should have been using for this new append-age of mine). And I'm supposed to be happy. Great. It's time to go—well, as soon as Gordon gets me dressed and out the door.

I'm pretty depressed as we leave. I don't know why; after all, Elaine was nice enough and informative. Something is niggling at me, and it has taken me down.

Sensing my mood, Gordon suggests that we go out for lunch before the appointment with Dr. Lewis. Really? A restaurant? It has been weeks since that has been possible, but instead of lifting my mood, all I think about is the diffi-culty of finding an easily accessible restaurant with seating that will work and foods I can eat. My footsteps down the hospital corridors get slower and slower. I'm miserable. Maybe it's because, without the support belt, I feel like my insides are going to fall out onto the floor.

As Gordon gets me into the car, he takes charge.

"We'll go to our favourite Japanese restaurant. Your udon noodle bowl was okay for you, yesterday, wasn't it? We know the tables and chairs in the open area should be fine for you, and we know you can manage the two steps down. Just you watch, I'll get parking right out front. I know it."

True to his word, there is a parking spot right in front.

It seems really extravagant to do this, but I order my fa-vourite bento lunch box. It will be far too much food, but the thought of having a bite or two of tempura, and some chicken teriyaki, and even some sashimi actually does lift my spirits. The waitress kindly substitutes some noodles for the rice and a piece each of salmon and tuna sashimi for the sushi rolls that are usually included.

Gordon grins at my anticipation of lunch. He's so pleased that my funk is easing.

I'm embarrassed to ask for a knife and fork when our food arrives. I know that chopsticks are beyond me right now. My fingers are best for the tempura and the sashimi, but noodles and teriyaki need utensils.

The prawn tempura is silky, delicious. The yam tempura is soft, sweet. Both are familiar special treats, and they both make my mouth water. I eat them both, leaving not a trace. As I usually do, I save my nibbles of salmon and tuna sashimi for dessert, if I have room. But I can only manage a couple of bites of teriyaki before I'm too full. Sadly, I watch Gordon take the remaining choice morsels and add them to his bento box. At least I know that my aversion to seafood is disappearing!

We linger over green tea for a while, both of us glad to be out, together. But soon it is time for the appointment with Dr. Lewis.

His office is the most efficient, pleasant doctor's office I've ever experienced. Carmen greets us by name as we walk in, introduces herself, and then explains how long we can expect to wait. Sure enough, within moments of her predicted time, we are escorted into an examining room, where we expect to wait for a while. Not at all. Dr. Lewis comes in almost immediately, carrying his laptop and a file folder of paper.

He sees a purple file folder in Gordon's hand, and asks, "Is that for me?"

Gordon replies, "These are the charts and discharge papers from the hospital in Empoli. I've made copies for you if you would like them. Some are in Italian; others are in English."

"That's terrific. I'll have Carmen add them to your file, but I do have them on my computer as well, from the hospital, including the translated versions."

Well—that's pretty efficient!

"I'm sure you have questions, but let's go over the test results first, so that you have the same information that I do for any discussions we might have.

"Considering the rough time you've had, you are in remarkably good shape. You don't have any trace of infection left, and no fever. You still have some fluid hanging around your lungs, but I'm not overly concerned about it. It should gradually disappear as you become more active. Your liver enzymes are not perfect. Again, I'm not overly concerned because that often happens after such a serious infection. We'll keep watch on the fluid and the enzymes, though, of course.

"I want to check your incision and the ostomy again. You can just climb up onto the bed and inch your waistband down. You don't need to get undressed."

Once again, I'm filled with disbelief. Why in hell's name don't people realize that when your stomach muscles have been cut apart, you can't do simple things like "climb up onto the bed"? Gordon, seeing what's going on in my mind, gives me "the button your lip" look, and then moves over to help me onto the bed.

Dr. Lewis doesn't seem to notice. "Elaine took those stitches out this morning?"

"Yes."

"Good. It was past time for them to come out. She also took a suture out from your incision. Was it here?"

"Yes."

"It looks fine. It would have dissolved over time, but she felt it was irritating you. Okay, I'm ready for your questions now. Let's take our time and make sure you have all the information you need. You go through them in the order that is important to you."

"Last night, Sandy Logan, our physiotherapist on Bowen—"

He interrupts, "Oh, I know her. She is very good."

"Yes, she is wonderful. She came to our home last night to help us figure out how to get me in and out of bed without the risk of injuring Gordon. As usual, she was very thorough, checking me out fully. She asked me if I had any pain that I hadn't reported. When I told her that I had leg pain, she said I should tell you, that you might want to get an ultrasound done on it."

Dr. Lewis becomes very alert. "Where is the pain?"

"In my left calf, just below my knee."

"Can you describe the pain?"

"It's there all the time. It's deep down. It's constant, not throbbing. Kind of a burning sensation but not tingling."

"How long have you had it?"

"Since I woke up after surgery."

"Did you tell anyone about it?"

"No. It just didn't seem important with all that was going on."

"Well, Sandy is correct. I want an ultrasound done immediately." He leaves and comes back right away. "Carmen is making the arrangements with the hospital now. When you leave I want you to go to the radiology department. If there's a problem, you'll need to stay until we figure out what to do." Dr. Lewis continues, "Well, I didn't expect that concern! Do you have others?"

"Yes. When can I get the resection done? I'm worried. I know that it is difficult getting surgical times, and, according to the doctors in Italy, the best timing is to have the surgery done is within the next two weeks."

"Hmm."

I'm beginning to hate the "Hmm" response from medical folks. The niggling returns, accompanied by anxiety.

"I generally do resections no earlier than three to four months after the first surgery. Sometimes as long as nine months, even a year."

My anxiety has just increased to panic. "A year? How can the bowel resume its function after that long?"

"The body is truly amazing. Don't worry, you are recovering very well. But you are still weak, and I want you much stronger before performing the resection."

"Well, if you generally do it after three to four months, that would be in early January. Can we plan on that?"

"We'll see. I'm not in a rush."

He might not be in a rush, but I am. I want this all behind me. Now!

Before I can express my frustration, Gordon interjects with his concern.

"When reviewing Joyce's file with me before we left, Dr. Lollio mentioned that they had noticed a possible abnormality that he would have investigated ahead of doing a resection. He mentioned an endoscopy."

"I'll review the notes from Italy very carefully, I promise. My colleagues in Italy appear to have been thorough, and I will be respectful of their observations. We can talk further about what will need to be done before the next surgery. By the way, what happened to your voice?"

Before I can answer, Carmen knocks on the door. She gives us her generous smile and says, "They can take you in a half hour in radiology. They've had a cancellation. I let them know that you have to get back home to the island tonight, and the last ferry is at nine thirty."

We hurry to make the appointment. Well, "hurry" is hardly the word when it involves me and getting in and out of a car.

We wait for hours. The waiting room fills up, then empties. Finally, my name is called. I'm led to the room where the ultrasound equipment is housed, then once again hear the idiotic suggestion to "just lie down on that bed." For once, the bed isn't chest-high, so I can actually sit on it. But lying down is *not possible. I don't have any stomach muscles to lower myself, and I don't have arm strength to support myself either!!* I am screaming the words inside but manage to be polite enough to the technician. He truly seems surprised, and quite unused to helping. I actually have to tell him what to do: first swing my legs onto the bed, and then support me as I lie down.

"So Dr. Lewis thinks we have a clot somewhere in our left leg?"

I'm not sure when I offered shared ownership of my leg, but I nod.

"Well, we had better find out—right away. That could be serious."

He doesn't ask where the pain is. He starts scanning up by my groin.

"The pain is in my calf."

"I like to make sure we know what we have and where we have it," he says with pride of ownership. "Hmm."

There's that new medical term again—the one I don't like much. It's odd, too. He's scanning the outside of my calf, but the pain is on the inside.

Out he goes. When he comes back, he says, "The radiologist wants to speak to the internal medicine specialist who is on call. It might take a while, so you should go back out to the waiting room. They'll let you know where to go from there."

Oh, great! I so want to yell: "*I couldn't lie down. How do you expect me to get up?*" Luckily, I catch his attention before he bustles out and politely ask for help. Temper control is becoming an issue for me.

We wait some more. Then the receptionist for the radiology department comes over to let us know that because the regular hours are over, we need to go to the emergency ward to wait. She has called for a wheelchair for me.

"A wheelchair?"

"Yes, the radiologist doesn't think that it is a good idea for you to be walking around."

So, I guess I know what that means: I do have a deep-vein thrombosis—a clot in my leg that could dislodge and travel to my lungs, causing a pulmonary embolism—a blockage that is potentially fatal. It is relatively common after surgery, particularly when a patient can't get moving soon after. And that means that I'm going to have to take anticoagulants to dissolve it. And that means no surgery until it is gone.

Strangely, the niggling sensation is gone. I'm always better when I know the truth rather than living with guesses. I know the specialist hasn't confirmed the presence of a clot, but the concern about me walking is a good enough indicator.

So we return to the secure cocoon of the emergency ward, back to the same little cubicle of yesterday.

"It's way past suppertime. Why don't you at least go to the cafeteria for something," I suggest to Gordon. "You've got the cellphone. They can call you."

"Are you sure?"

"Yes. The muscle spasms are back. I need some rest."

"I'm going to ask them for some medication for the muscle spasms. They have that on your chart. It shouldn't be a problem."

"Okay. But then go."

He's worked magic with the doctor. A nurse arrives with medication, speaking as she enters the cubicle, "We don't have exactly the same product you received in Italy, but the pharmacist says—"

She doesn't complete her thought, but then says, "Oh, you poor dear, you look like you are in a lot of pain. No wonder you need this. I'll get you a warm blanket to lie on. That should help as well."

Gradually, the medication kicks in and I can rest. I try to sink into the mattress as deeply as I can, relaxing every part of me. I'm exhausted.

"Hello! I'm Dr. McLeod! I'm the internal medicine doctor on call tonight! You've been waiting around for me! Sorry I've been so long! I've been in surgery all afternoon! Lots of emergencies today! I've got your ultrasound results here! Let's see what we have!"

He's young. He's lean. He's intense. Is he taking ownership of my leg, too?

"Hmm. No question. You have a blood clot. It's a good thing it is lodged where it is. If it had been higher, it could have been a problem on your flight home. By the way, you've had quite the time of it, haven't you? Well, I have to put you on an anticoagulant. We need the clot to dissolve. Over time, it would dissolve on its own, probably, but it's preferable to nudge the dissolving along with drugs—especially since you've got another surgery coming up. Let's go over our choices of drugs, shall we?"

Well, this is better. The "we" in his sentences conveys that "we" are a team, making decisions together. Okay, I'll play along.

"So what are our choices?" I ask.

"Well, of course there is Warfarin, but the trouble with that is it takes a long time to ease off it. Then there are some newer drugs, but each has its limitations. There is a very new drug that I think could work well for you, but it is quite expensive. Do you have an extended health care plan?"

"I do have one, but how long will I have to be on the drug?"

"Three months."

"I guess that means no surgery for three months, then."

"Absolutely no surgery, unless it is an emergency. But that is one of the advantages of this drug. You can have surgery within three days of stopping it, and there is no easing-off period. That's why I think it would work for you—plus, there are minimal side effects."

"When do you think I could have the surgery?"

"This is mid-October. So mid-November, mid-December, mid-January. I'd say late January would be okay."

"Could you please let Dr. Lewis know? I really want to get it scheduled now. I was hoping to have the surgery next month. I hate this ostomy!"

"I can't promise what Dr. Lewis will do, but he will get my report. I understand you live on Bowen?"

"Yes."

"Is there a pharmacy on the island?"

"Yes."

"Good! They may not have this drug yet, but they'll be able to order it! Oh, I just realized—this is Friday! They won't be able to get it until Monday! You need to start it now! I'm going to give you an injection of it here, but you need pills starting tomorrow! Maybe you should pick up the prescription in North Vancouver before you go! When does the last ferry leave?"

"Nine thirty."

"You don't have time. I'll run over to my office to get a sample package for you! But first, here's the injection!"

Fortunately, he doesn't give injections with the same intensity that he speaks, but I'm pretty sure he is running to his office.

Gordon comes in. He's ready to book a hotel room for the night, but I explain that we can probably make the ferry. It usually isn't full at nine thirty, and we should be able to leave soon. We agree that he'll go and get the car, bring it round to the ER door, and wait for me there. I'm sure Dr. McLeod will arrange for someone to get me out to meet up with him.

His office must be close. I don't think I've waited more than five minutes. He's carrying two sample packages of the drug.

"I thought it best to make sure you had several days' worth! But do go to your pharmacy right away to make sure they can get stock! How are you getting home? You're not driving, are you?"

When I start to explain that Gordon has gone to get the car, he interrupts. "I'll go and get an orderly and a wheelchair! You look exhausted! You need to make that ferry! Goodbye! Good luck! I hope I don't have to see you again!"

Within seconds, I am in a wheelchair and being pushed down the corridor to Gordon and our car. When I'm buckled in, I feel like I've just been picked up by a tornado, whirled around, and settled back down again.

Like magic, we arrive at the ferry terminal and drive right onto the waiting ferry.

I'm going to bed as soon as we get home, and I'm *not* going anywhere tomorrow!

20

OCTOBER 12

————

THE RINGING phone wakes me from a deep sleep. I look over to our king-size bed to see if Gordon has heard the phone. He's not there. Now I notice the light coming through the windows. Although it's cloudy, I can see the sun is in the south already—it must be late in the morning!

I can hear Gordon's voice coming up from his study. This is a long phone call. Yikes! The diaper was dry when I woke up, but I really need to pee. Hopefully, he'll come up and get me out of bed as soon as the call is over. It would be so great to make it through the night without a wet diaper.

No sooner does he hang up than the phone rings again. I can't hold it any longer. The diaper becomes my external bladder, bulging, squishy. But at least the bed isn't wet. At my Monday appointment with Sandy I *have* to learn how to get in and out of bed on my own. This is *crazy*.

Finally, I hear his footsteps on the stairs. He peeks in and sees me awake.

"Sorry. The word is out that we are home. I guess we can expect a lot of calls. People want to know how you are. The first call was Marnie. She's home and wants to see you right away. Gibson has been away from us for too long, so I'd like to pick him up from the dog ranch this afternoon. Marnie will come for her visit while I'm out. Is that okay?"

"As long as I don't have to go anywhere, that's fine. I'm really glad Marnie can come today. I *need* to talk to her."

At this last comment, Gordon looks surprised. He doesn't know anything about my promise to Philip. He doesn't say anything, though. He can see the determined look on my face.

"I'm concerned about Gibson, though," I say.

"I know you are worried that he's going to be rambunctious around you, but you know that he doesn't have a mean bone in his body. He's a golden retriever! He's a gentle soul, and I'm quite sure that after an initial sniff, he'll figure out that you need his protection. I wouldn't be surprised if he comes in, lies down beside you, and doesn't move."

I also know that we can't leave him at the dog ranch forever. I guess now is as good a time as any.

"Wow—you really had to pee last night!"

"Actually, it was while you were on the phone. I was dry until then." Oh darn, that isn't fair to the guy—he has been so patient with me. "Sorry—that came out pretty grouchy."

"A bit," he says, helping me out of bed. "It's 11:00 a.m. Do you want breakfast or lunch?"

"Lunch would be good. I'd love some of my homemade chicken-and-rice soup. There are a couple of packages of it in the freezer. Would you make that for me, please?"

"Well, that's easy to do. I wasn't sure what we had that would work. You haven't been eating much at all."

"I know. I think I've lost close to thirty pounds. For the first time in my life, I'm all skin and bones—rather like a corpse."

"Are you sure that the rice will be okay? You didn't want rice with the teriyaki yesterday."

"The rice in the soup is soft from so much cooking. I'm sure it will be okay."

And the soup tastes delicious. Since foods were reintroduced into my diet, I've wanted soup. I don't understand why it wasn't part of the meal plan in the hospital—it can be so nutritious. Except for a disastrous lentil/pea/bean soup we tried for our last lunch at Santa Maria, and the udon noodle soup the other day, soup hasn't been available. I'm glad I made a batch before we left—I figured it would be handy if we were tired and hungry when we got back. Little did I know!

"Gordon, could you leave before Marnie gets here? I need a little time to myself."

"Are you sure that you'll be okay on your own?"

"I'll be fine, and Marnie will be here soon. It will be good for me."

He looks at me carefully. "Are you all right? You look tense."

"I'm fine. I need to collect my thoughts."

What I want to say is, "I need to prepare myself. This is going to be a very, very emotional conversation for Marnie—for both of us. It could end our friendship. Or it could bond us together forever. I'll be telling her something I haven't even shared with you, yet. I've been keeping a secret from you, and that hasn't felt good, especially because it is about the most extraordinary experience of my life." I don't say any of this, but I can tell that Gordon knows I'm holding back.

"I'll leave at twelve forty-five, then, if that works for you."

"Thank you."

He isn't gone for long before I hear Marnie's car. I wish she would replace her old station wagon. I keep asking her if the brakes are okay, and she always says they are. But they squeak dreadfully, especially as she comes down our steep driveway. I'm sure they're not safe.

She knocks, then comes in without waiting for me to open it. I'm only a few feet away by this time.

"Oh! You're *up*! And *dressed*! Why aren't you in bed? You've been so dreadfully sick!"

Surprise at seeing me standing near the door is replaced by shock at my appearance. She falls silent.

"Oh, you poor dear. You look so weak."

We walk to the living room. She can see the rocking chair has been set up for me—it has new cushions and the upholstered footstool is in front of it for my feet. Gordon has lit a small fire. The room is cozy. After she settles me into the rocking chair, she bustles into the kitchen to finish preparing the tea makings that are there. We're silent through this. She needs time to recover from the sight of me. I need to gather strength for my story.

She hands me a mug of tea, then chooses my favourite chair—the one that has lost its footstool mate.

Leaning forward, she says, "I am so sorry I couldn't get to you in Italy. I tried and tried, but the travel arrangements were just too difficult, especially as I was trying to make them while in Hungary. It just couldn't be done."

I respond with the first words she has heard from me today: "Thank you for trying, but it is probably just as well. There wasn't much you could have done for us."

She looks at me with astonishment. "Whatever has happened to your voice? Do you have a cold on top of everything else? What else can go wrong?"

"I don't have a cold. I ripped the nasogastric tube out when I was having a hallucination. No one seems to know what has been damaged. There was lots of blood, so I imagine some healing is needed."

We both take a sip of tea. With her head bowed, she slowly shakes her head. "I was so worried about you. I thought I was going to lose you, too. I couldn't bear the thought. That's why I wanted to come. I'm so glad you're home—but oh my, you've a long way to go to being better, I can see that. How did this happen? Do you know why? What happened?"

"Marnie, we don't know how or why it happened. The doctors asked if I had eaten any seafood, so I guess they thought I might have swallowed a bone or something. But I hadn't. And I had a colonoscopy in July. I was given a clean bill of health. We just don't know. It will remain a mystery, I guess. As to what happened, well, on our second morning in Tuscany all of a sudden..." I try to keep my story as short as I can, but it still takes a few minutes to describe the events leading up to surgery.

At that point, Marnie interjects, "I can see you're fading. Let me help you get to bed and I'll wait until Gordon gets back."

"No, Marnie. I have a promise to keep. I came back with a message for you—from Philip."

Shock. Disbelief. Confusion. Her emotions race across her face. "From Philip?" she says, her voice rising with each syllable.

"Yes. It might take me a while to tell it, and it will be hard for me to tell you. Could you move closer so that you can hear me? My voice is fading."

She moves to sit beside my feet on the footstool, then folds my hands in hers. "Tell me." Her own voice is tight with emotion and wavering in a whisper.

"I'm not sure I've ever told you, but over the years I've had a number of out-of-body experiences. As a child, it was an escape route, and I really didn't know what I was doing. Then as an adult, when studying East/West medicine and meditating, I had others. In every experience, I was surrounded by the presence of an abiding love, and the light around me was a warm, dark purple. I tell you this now because what I experienced in Italy was far more profound. I was near death."

For a moment, her hands grip mine, then relax back into her soft holding.

"The first time—"

"The first? There was more than one?" she says, interrupting.

"Yes, Philip was with me four times."

"Oh." The word is a quiet wail. I know it is a reflection of the grief she holds so tightly within her.

"The first time it happened was when I was in surgery. I was such a fool to believe that the acute pain I was in all day would go away, especially because I know that I have a high pain threshold. So when I got to surgery, not only did I have a perforated bowel that had to be repaired, but I was also filled with the contents of my bowel. It was everywhere around my organs. The combination of everything made it touch and go as to whether or not I lived. I think I'd had enough, and found my escape route.

"But I kind of flew through the warm purple light, going further than I had ever gone before. Seeing a glow, I stopped to watch. Sort of a curtain lifted. Behind it lay the most beautiful place I have ever seen. A place of warm, pulsating, glowing, silvery-golden white light. A place of glorious peace and wholeness and silence. A place I have always longed to be."

Even as I'm telling Marnie this, I can hear my father's benediction again: "May the peace that passeth all understanding be with you now and forevermore. Amen."

I continue, "Although I knew I would be welcome, I didn't approach. Instead, I drew in the love that surrounded me from all those who were there. In front of me were several 'ones who have gone before.' Their backs were toward me. They were filled with that warm, pulsating white light.

"One turned just his head fully toward me, without moving the rest of his body. It was Philip. His right hand was raised. He moved his index finger side to side—just once. And he filled me with knowledge, for there is no spoken language in that place, only shared comprehension: 'Now is not your time. You have a choice, but you don't have to be here. I ask that you choose to live, and take a message to Marnie. Tell her that it *was* my time. I had no choice. Tell her that I love her and have always loved her. And tell her that I will always be with her. Help her understand what you see here, and how it is possible for me to be with her, always.'

"Philip knew me. Ever the volunteer, ever willing to help others, I sadly, reluctantly turned away from that place of wonder and returned to my ravaged body."

We are both weeping. My voice has faded so much that she is leaning forward, almost touching her head against my chest so that she can hear.

She looks at me. "Why didn't he talk to me before he died? Why? I tried to get him to talk, but he wouldn't admit how sick he was. Why?"

"I don't know, Marnie. All I know is that he loved you so much he found a way to tell you after he died. Surely, that is a rare gift."

"But why did he tell *you*? Why didn't he tell *me*?"

"I was worried you might feel that way. Maybe because I was there?"

There is a long silence. We both need time. We sit, holding each other, tears streaming down our faces. I ask for more tea, as much to give us time as to get the liquid.

She returns with tea for us both. "You said there were four times. Can you tell me the others?"

I nod.

"The second time was during one of my morphine hallucinations. I tried so hard but could not fight off the effects of the drugs. Again and again, I was drawn under, thrashing fruitlessly against my bed restraints that reinforced the fear of being held against my will. I was in a hell where prison guards and ghostly figures imposed their will against mine, and where a double-headed dragon observed this struggle with glee, waiting for its chance to attack. I could not breathe. My heart pounded with my struggle and my fear. I had to escape. So I left my body.

"The deep purple of the beyond was there to embrace me once again. I was alone but not afraid. I knew that space is devoid of life as we know it, but it is not empty. It has an energy of its own—a spiritual energy that soothes. I remained there for a long time, then noticed a warm glow. It was Philip's energy, surrounded by the familiar energy of others whom I could not identify. Philip's message was brief: 'You promised me that you would choose to live. It is time to return.' The loving energy accompanied me back to my body but no further."

"He came to protect you!"

"Yes, and to remind me of my promise. The third time was very brief. It happened the night the fluid around my lungs got out of control. That night, I felt like I was drowning. I guess I was—in my own fluids. This time the loving light was waiting for me nearby, enveloping me as I emerged into it. I was swaddled among them—the faceless bearers of light and love. They enfolded me, allowing me to be among them for a while but not forever. This time, they returned with me to hover over me—I continued to feel their presence for a long while."

"He came to comfort you!"

"Yes, and to escort me back to make sure I kept my promise. The fourth time was the first night back in the apartment at Santa Maria. I had been thinking of Philip's memorial service and realized that I should plan my own. So I did, right then, lying in bed. When I was finished, I was completely at peace, satisfied that my life had been well spent, knowing that it was fine for me to leave. In another dimension, I could see myself holding shimmering scissors in my hand. I was ready to sever the silver thread that binds me to earthly existence. As I reached up to sever the thread, Philip appeared. His presence wasn't as clear as before, but I could still tell it was him. 'You daft silly,' he said, 'what's the point of preparing that beautiful memorial service if you don't tell anyone about it?' I felt the warmth of a touch. 'Besides, you have a promise to keep, don't you?' Then he was gone. Alone, I still could see the silver thread, and then I realized I no longer had the shimmering scissors. They had disappeared."

"'Daft silly'! That sounds like something he would say!"

It is that phrase, "daft silly," that finally convinces her, I think. And with that, I can see she is gathering strength from Philip's love.

Marnie finds her voice. "I feel like a weight around my heart has been lifted. Thank you, my dear, dear friend. This has been such a burden for you but such a gift for me. I need to go home now. I need to be alone with my memories, but this time without the bitterness I've tasted. You've given me so much to think about, and already you have given me some peace."

"Marnie—Philip gave you that. It was from him."

Tears form again with my words, and she cannot reply. As she nods, she squeezes her eyes, wringing the tears out.

Her face reveals both sorrow and joy. I know there will be many tears for her tonight. It will be a full moon in a clear sky. Philip died the night of a full moon, and each month since his death in June, that shining orb in the night sky has been a vivid reminder of the full life they had together and the loss of her soulmate. May her healing begin tonight.

She gets up quietly, hugs me gently, and leaves.

The front door closes silently behind her, my promise kept. As the quiet settles around me, love and peace fill me anew—and a longing for that place that will be home someday. Until then, I am different than I was. There is a new sense of purpose, as yet undefined. A new journey begins.

AFTERWORD

O N JANUARY 26, 2013, Dr. Lewis performed the resection of the ileostomy. Ten days later, I sent out a celebratory message to those who would appreciate the two words: "I pooped!"

Regaining strength and stamina, though, took three years and the expert teamwork of my rehabilitation trinity: Sandy Logan, physiotherapist; Mary Letson, personal trainer; and Mary McDonagh, massage therapist. Without them, I would never have returned to the joys of my active life—gardening, canoeing, walking Gibson on forest trails, keeping up with Ella and Finn. There were several bumps along the way, including the development of adhesions in my abdominal cavity, which caused massive spasms and rendered me helpless. Not good to have one of those while driving!

One day, as I was massaging vitamin E oil onto my scar, I noticed that it was becoming less red and cord-like.

"Do you want to see my scar?" I asked Gordon, lifting my shirt.

Silence. Then, "That's the most beautiful scar I have ever seen," he said, eyes brimming with tears.

With those words, the spectre of the ileostomy vanished, along with any lingering psychological scars.

Sadly, my voice has not completely returned, and I can no longer sing.

As to my spiritual journey, it has taken unanticipated turns. After I told Marnie what had happened with Philip, I felt compelled to share it with others.

In the fall of 2013, I was visiting my friend Lael. She was in the late stages of cancer, facing death, and was feeling anxious. It just seemed right to share with her what had happened to me in Italy.

At the end of my story, she said, "So, there is nothing to fear about death?"

"No. It is the dying part that can be awful. Death brings beauty, peace, light, love beyond comprehension."

She said, "Thank you. I wanted to believe that, but I've been seeking reassurance. I trust you, and know that you would only tell me what you know to be true. I can hardly wait until Bill comes home so that I can tell him. It will help him, too."

And then she said in her gravelly voice, "My dear, you must write a book about your experience. I know it will help others."

In 2013, I resumed my volunteer work and used every opportunity to honour the promise I made to help children's voices be heard. My proudest moment was when four children joined me on the podium during my keynote speech at the 2014 inauguration of Bowen Island's newly elected municipal council. The children described the values they expected elected officials to uphold: justice, honesty, gratitude, responsibility. They were serious about it. Their wisdom has had a profound effect on the council and on the community.

Tuscany beckoned us again in September 2015. We resumed our twenty-fifth anniversary trip where it had been interrupted, welcomed as family members by Laura, Stefania, and Giuseppe at Santa Maria. This was made even more special when Clara, now three, shyly introduced her baby sister, Sophie.

Our apartment at Santa Maria was the same one we had initially—up the twenty steps. We felt like we had come home.

Knowing that I needed closure, on the first day Gordon drove me over the mountain road to the hospital in Empoli. As we drove, we shared memories of the previous drive. I remembered the slipping and sliding I had done in the ambulance. No wonder! The road is narrow with twists and turns, ups and downs. Gordon remembered following the brake lights of the ambulance, relying on them as his beacon. Once he was over the mountain, though, he lost sight of them; the ambulance was able to speed through the little towns. He had to rely on instinct—his fear for me, his need to be with me, giving him confidence as he chose which way to go. Maybe I was his beacon. He drove directly to the hospital without a single wrong turn!

When we got to Empoli, we parked on a street and walked to the hospital. I stood at the entrance, looking up at this beautiful new structure. It was eerie. I had spent thirteen days of my life inside but had no idea what it looked like on the outside. It was not at all familiar to me.

The eerie feeling continued as we walked through the reception area to the double doors of the intensive care unit. The doors were closed. Two women were there, clinging to one another, giving each other courage to face whatever awaited them on the other side. A loved one was inside. There was nothing they could do but wait. This is what Gordon had done, by himself. His anxiety must have been immense—too much. But somehow he found the strength to cope, and I am so grateful.

Respecting their need for privacy, we left and went to the third floor, in search of "my" room. At last, this was familiar! The corridors were wide and sparkling clean, the configuration exactly as I remembered. And then—yes—there was "my" room, but I only took a quick glance; I felt like an intruder. Suddenly, Claudia was there, wanting to know what we were doing there. She must have thought we were intruders, too. There was quite a commotion as she realized that we didn't speak Italian, but fortunately Dr. Lollio arrived at that very moment. After introductions, Claudia relaxed a bit but not entirely, until Salvadore arrived. He recognized us immediately. They all were delighted to see me looking so healthy, and Gordon without the weight of the world on his shoulders. It was nice, simple closure.

Later that evening, we were delighted to host dinner for Dr. Bing and Dr. Lollio. Imagine! A Saturday night and they were prepared to leave their families so that we could say thank you. It was a wonderful evening, made even more special because it was at a locally known restaurant, one that we would never have found on our own. Grilled baby squid with plenty of garlic—delicious!

For two weeks, we explored the back roads of Tuscany, enjoying the small colourful villages and the surrounding historical cities, indulging in gelato, espresso, pizza, and a taste of wild boar along the way (and a little wine).

On the last night of our trip, Laura held a cooking class, just for us. The menu for the dinner we created: crisp fried zucchini blossoms, picante tomato soup, handmade fettuccine with pesto sauce (the basil leaves picked from the pots on the windowsill), and tiramisu (in it was espresso made in a miniature espresso pot). As we cooked, we learned that Santa Maria was named for Laura's grandmother, the person who brought Laura's love of cooking to life. We toasted

Laura on her recent marriage to Simone. We had fun. The result was delicious, a perfect way to end our long drawn-out twenty-fifth wedding anniversary celebration.

Endings lead to reflection. I feel privileged to have had a glimpse of what lies beyond. And I am honoured that Philip trusted me to carry his message to Marnie. I hope my story will help you on your life's journey as you struggle with vulnerability and confront death. It is so important to admit our vulnerability and express our love in this life. Philip was lucky—even after death, he had a chance to do both.

THANK YOU *for joining me. As we walk this universal space, the web of life reveals itself, throbbing with possibilities. Each action, each choice rippling out, creating a living memory for time immemorial—our true legacy. What will our legacy be? Will it be hope, love, fear, anger, complacency, compassion, wisdom? Our legacy, our choice. Here we are linked to the past, we create the present, and we give to the future. Here we are more than ourselves. Here we are all one.*

ACKNOWLEDGEMENTS

To Gordon for his love, fierce determination, and willingness for me to share our story.

To my family and friends for holding me in their circle of love.

To Michelle, who made it possible for me to pursue my dream of writing.

To Dr. Bing and Dr. Lollio for saving my life.

To the staff of Saint Giuseppe's Hospital in Empoli for their caring and their professionalism.

To Laura and Stefania for making us feel at home at Santa Maria.

To Dr. Lewis and Dr. McLeod for the competent transition of my health care at home.

To Marnie for allowing Philip's story to be told.

To all those who agreed to have their names included.

To Diane for her wise, steady, loving counsel.

To Shirarose Wilensky, gentle, probing editor.

To Jesse Finkelstein for guiding the publishing process.

Unless individuals have given approval for their real names to be included, I have substituted names. If names have been used that are similar or the same as real ones, it was done inadvertently and I apologize.

ABOUT THE AUTHOR

JOYCE GANONG has been writing all of her life, but this is her first book.

Fascinated by stories told by international visitors to her family's dinner table, she began her own travels at age twenty-one as a volunteer teacher in Tanzania. Her letters from Africa echoed that ancient thrum of life—her way of sharing her experiences with family and friends, and introducing them to the unfamiliar.

Africa anchored Joyce's awareness of the importance of nutrition. Returning to Canada, she earned a Master of Science degree in Human Nutrition. Again, she wanted to share her knowledge and was at the forefront of nutrition education, developing food and nutrition teaching tools to engage students in the delicious art of eating well. Her articles on health and wellness appeared in national and local publications, including *Canadian Living* and *B.C. Runner.*

Joyce's passion for building community has been widely recognized; she is recipient of a Rotary Integrity Award and the Queen's Golden Jubilee Medal for her community service, among other accolades.

When she's not writing, Joyce spends time with her husband, Gordon, her two daughters, and grandchildren, and she continues to volunteer. She served as Co-Chair of Vital Conversations, now a national initiative of the Community Foundations of Canada. She lives on Bowen Island, B.C.